properly before you settle d[own]

[ti]mes as carefully as you ch[oose]

[ ] as important to you to enjoy

[ ]

[ ] do in a theatre or concert hall.

[prog]ramme if your mind is wandering

[re]ading. Give it your full attention.

[y]our eye is not caught by familiar

[ac]tion will be twice as vivid. If you

[hav]en't a right to criticize.

[   ]tion. Don't you like a change

[re]st now and then.

'Good Listening', from an article in the *BBC Yearbook 1930*

The Story of Broadcasting House
Home of the BBC

The Story of Broadcasting House
Home of the BBC

Mark Hines

Photography by Tim Crocker
Foreword by Sir Terry Wogan

MERRELL
LONDON · NEW YORK
in association with the BBC

Contents

Foreword   6

Introduction   8

The Birth of the BBC   10

The Building of Broadcasting House   20

Broadcasting House in the 1930s   36

A Tour of Broadcasting House in the Early 1930s   54

Broadcasting House Comes of Age   94

'Once Breathtaking, Now Comforting'   112

A Digital Voice   122

A Tour of Broadcasting House in 2007   144

Sources   188

Acknowledgements   189

Index   189

Picture Credits   192

There she sits, the grand old lady of broadcasting, stately as a galleon, abutting Portland Place like a colossus; and for a lately arrived boy broadcaster, the fulfilment of an impossible dream. Only someone for whom the BBC was a light shining in the darkness, a window on another, greater world outside a small Irish town, will understand the frisson, the thrill of excitement and apprehension of that first time I walked through those mighty bronze doors into the great temple itself. For that's what it was to me, and always will be: a cathedral, a Sistine Chapel; sacred, hallowed ground. Don't tell me that the ghost of Great Reith does not yet abide in this spare, Art Deco hall, as I walk in the footsteps of a thousand great broadcasters. 'Nation Shall Speak Peace Unto Nation.' Not the Auntie, but the Mother and Father of all the world's broadcasters, the template by which they're all measured. And I'm part of it .... Of course, with the passing of time, I've taken liberties with the old girl, but the awestruck feeling – the sense of how incredibly lucky I am to wander Broadcasting House's endless corridors, inevitably ending up where I started – has never really left me.

The past few years have brought great change to the BBC, inside and out, but *plus ça change* ...: the great ship of broadcasting doesn't look any different to me. She's had a complete refurbishment, she's brighter, airier, with a lighter swing to her petticoats than before, but she remains what she always was to a small boy huddled by a wireless in a little house in an Irish town: the gateway to the stars.

Sir Terry Wogan, KBE

THE RADIO TIMES

Broadcasting House Number.   Price 2d.

The iconic image of Broadcasting House has been used for more than seventy-five years to represent the home of the BBC.

In the mid-1930s Michael Carr's 'Regent Street Rhapsody' was performed for the first time by Geraldo and His Orchestra. The composition tells the story of a young playboy who leaves a smoky nightclub at the top of Regent Street and suddenly becomes aware of his wastrel life. Glancing up from the deserted pavement, he is captivated by the shimmering white façade of Broadcasting House in the early-morning haze. In the 1980s, as a student, I would often pass by Broadcasting House (or 'BH', as it is known within the BBC), although usually at a more civilized time of day. I would occasionally try to get a glimpse inside, but I never once dared enter through its imposing bronze doors. Broadcasting House seemed mysterious, inaccessible and forbidding, but at the same time elegant, comforting and reassuring. In my mind it conjured up images of presenters in evening dress, speaking in those clipped 1930s tones. I imagined the radio mast on the roof broadcasting to the world. To me, Broadcasting House was the BBC.

This book offers a glimpse behind those heavy doors. To be inside Broadcasting House today is to get a sense of the original pioneering spirit, chaos, excitement and controlled terror that comes with live broadcast, mixed with the mundane reality of day-to-day life in a monolithic organization. This is an institution that is part of our collective memory. It was from here that *Today* woke us up, shipping forecasts warned us of gales in the Outer Hebrides, and underground cables allowed Princess Elizabeth and Winston Churchill to speak to the country during the Blitz. The walls of Broadcasting House have literally soaked up these sounds for more than seventy-five years. If it were ever the case that a building could speak, Broadcasting House would have a lot to say.

It has not always been this way. At the birth of the British Broadcasting Company in 1922, it was not at all clear that wireless broadcasting would catch on. However, early successes allowed the new company to outgrow its first proper accommodation at Savoy Hill at a phenomenal rate, and by 1927, as the BBC was transformed into the British Broadcasting Corporation, the search was on for a new home. By chance, a site on Portland Place not only became available, but also came complete with an architect. Out of the relationship between the BBC's newly appointed Director of Premises and civil engineer, Marmaduke Tudsbery, and its architect, Lieutenant-Colonel George Val Myer, Broadcasting House was born.

At the time of its opening in 1932, the building was hailed as a state-of-the-art 'sound factory': one of the first buildings in the world specially designed to make noise. But it had one foot in the past and one in the future. This was reflected in its architecture, which was both conservative and modern: it boasted the most modern architectural interiors in the country, while outside, Georgian-style windows helped the building to fit in with its surroundings. Eric Gill's sculptures hinted at the purpose of the building, and reflected the aspirations of the organization inside.

Broadcasting House may have started life as a 'sound factory', but it soon became home to the growing BBC. One early visitor called it the 'Big House'. Unfortunately, it was not quite big enough. Almost immediately after opening, the building destined to become a giant acoustic laboratory needed changes, and hammering and banging were often heard on air, as studios were rebuilt and staff moved around. Broadcasters have come and gone over the years, accompanied by generation after generation of builders.

Broadcasting House has seen many changes throughout its life. As the world of radio and television expanded the BBC moved more and more of its operation out of the building. In 1986 an exhibition at the Royal Academy referred to a patched-up Broadcasting House as 'hopelessly obsolete'. By the late 1990s a radical idea was beginning to form: to bring BBC News, Audio & Music and World Service together in one location. This was an opportunity to put Broadcasting House at the heart of the BBC's operation once more. The redevelopment would give the BBC greater civic presence, and expose the institution at work for the first time in its historic home.

The Story of Broadcasting House: Home of the BBC celebrates the completion in 2006 of one of London's most ambitious and complex conservation projects: the repair and conservation of Val Myer's Grade II*-listed building. It may not be obvious today, but after three years of careful repair and sympathetic new design work, Broadcasting House is now fully digital and no longer in danger of obsolescence.

As the project architect leading the repair and remodelling of Broadcasting House, I was captivated by the extraordinary history of the building and the wonderful work of architectural photographers Dell and Wainwright from the 1930s. This book was also a chance to bring the story up to date, and to make some comparisons between then and now. Broadcasting House has always been a working building of stark contrasts: a place where tradition is balanced with innovation, where panelled rooms sit alongside new studios, and where the BBC as both

institution and service has to balance its history with its present and future needs. Its very location on Regent Street is just at the point where the shopping stops and the serious institutions of Portland Place start.

In this book we can give only a partial glimpse of the organization that has spent a lifetime there. Broadcasting is a complicated business, and the BBC is, as we know, an extraordinary and complex institution. The very product made in this 'factory of sound' is not visible to the eye. Trying to capture this in a book has been a challenge, and I must thank Tim Crocker for his boundless energy, and his enthusiasm for attempting to photograph the invisible.

As I write, Broadcasting House looks much the same as it did when I ambled past as student, if a little cleaner. It is still a potent reminder in stone of the importance of the original ideas and aspirations of the BBC, a physical representation of the intangible. Broadcasting House shimmers once again in the early-morning light.

Mark Hines London, October 2007

1920

A short daily news service begins from Marconi's Wireless Telegraph Company's works in Chelmsford, Essex.

1922

18 October The British Broadcasting Company is formed.
1 November The first broadcast receiving licence is issued.
14 November First nightly transmissions of BBC programmes from 2LO transmitter on the roof of Marconi House. The office is located at nearby Magnet House.
14 December John Reith is appointed the Company's general manager.

1923

8 January The first outside broadcast is transmitted.
March Staff move into new premises at Savoy Place, on London's Embankment.
1 May The first studio in the Savoy Place building opens. The BBC continues to expand, and soon outgrows its accommodation.

1924

Expansion begins into the adjoining Savoy Hill building.

1925

The total number of licences sold reaches 200,000.

1926

Marmaduke Tudsbery joins the BBC as its civil engineer.

1927

1 January The British Broadcasting Company is granted a Royal Charter and becomes the British Broadcasting Corporation. Sir John Reith becomes the first Director-General.
26 July The BBC Control Board instructs Tudsbery to begin to search for an existing building that can be converted into a new headquarters building for the BBC. The Portland Place site is first drawn to the attention of the BBC in the early spring.

The Birth of the BBC

Above, left Dame Nellie Melba in Britain's first advertised public broadcast, singing from Marconi's works in Chelmsford.

Above, right John Reith, the driving force behind the early BBC, pictured in 1928. Reith set up an administration, assembled programmes that would attract an audience, trained performers, and built studios and transmitters. The early growth of his organization was phenomenal: within a year of his appointment the BBC staff had grown from 4 people to 177, and 5 stations had been added to those in London, Manchester and Birmingham.

Opposite In 1925 the London transmitter, on the roof of Marconi House, was replaced by a more powerful version, installed on the roof of Selfridges on Oxford Street. The new transmitter could reach as far as Luton, Godalming, Tunbridge Wells and Chelmsford.

In 1920 the hissing and crackling of the British ether was broken only by the occasional Morse signal. This was the year, though, that things began to change. A long-wave transmitter was installed at Marconi's Wireless Telegraph Company works in Chelmsford, Essex, enabling the transmission of a short daily news service and, later in the year, making it possible for the opera star Dame Nellie Melba to sing 'Home Sweet Home' over the airwaves. The strength of the transmitter had been doubled in time for the broadcast and, in theory at least, allowed her voice to be heard within a 1000-mile (1600-km) radius. Unfortunately, the station's licence was withdrawn a few months later because it was said that the transmissions were interfering with military communications. But, importantly, human voices had been carried further by wireless transmission than ever before.

Two years later, on Valentine's Day 1922, Marconi started transmitting programmes again, and on 11 May 1922 it opened a second station, 2LO, from its offices in London. It is estimated that by November that year about 30,000 people were listening to the two stations regularly. The success prompted interest from other companies, and the Post Office started receiving applications to set up other radio stations. Negotiations between the Post Office and representatives of various wireless manufacturers concluded that a single licence would be issued, provided that 'an adequate service could be guaranteed for a reasonable period of time'. The 'big six' manufacturers of wirelesses – Marconi, Metropolitan-Vickers, Radio Communication Company, Western Electric, General Electric and British Thomson-Houston – promised to deliver a broadcasting service for two years. In October, amid much speculation in the electrical press, it was

announced that they would jointly form the British Broadcasting Company Limited, and a small, temporary head office was established in Magnet House on Kingsway, in central London.

The chairman of the Formation Committee described the company's plans to *The Times*:

At the beginning, broadcasting will be conducted purely from a social point of view. Each evening, there will be given a brief synopsis of the world's news, prepared by four Press agencies who are acting together to supply the company. Then the Meteorological Department of the Air Ministry is supplying us, at first at any rate, with two weather reports. In addition to this news, there will be concerts, instrumental and vocal, and it may be that later we shall arrange for speeches written by popular people to be broadcast.

The first transmission of nightly 'BBC' programmes began on 14 November 1922, using the studio and 2LO transmitter on the roof of the nearby Marconi House. The studio was used as an office during the day, and had to be tidied up before the evening's programmes began. In his book *Broadcasting from Within*, C. Lewis described the small studio:

It contained a small desk and two telephones which had a perfect mania for ringing, and a typist who clicked away morning, noon and night. There were four microphones in the room, and the engineers could not leave them alone. They tapped them, shouted at them, coaxed them and whispered to them every minute of the day. They hung them here and then there … and treated them like a lot of spoiled children. And they insisted on silence in the room while they were doing it.

In these early days, about four hours of programmes were broadcast, although not always at the same time each day. Staff often had to make the short sprint down the road between their offices and the studio. Short singers had to stand on piles of books in order to reach the microphone, and programmes were occasionally interrupted with a polite apology: 'Just one moment please', or 'There will be an interval of three minutes while we move the piano.' Working for the youthful BBC clearly required a capacity for improvisation. An early employee recalled surviving on an evening diet of nothing but 'meringues and beer'.

Savoy Hill

While staff struggled to make the evening's programmes, the BBC's newly appointed General Manager, thirty-three-year-old John Reith, was searching for more suitable premises. Reith (1889–1971) visited the premises of the Institution of Electrical Engineers on Savoy Hill on London's Embankment. Despite having some trouble finding both the building's side door and its caretaker, he identified some unused space on the third floor. The offices were initially unpromising in appearance, but there seemed to be lots of room, so he decided to take the whole of the west wing of the building. By late March 1923 a handful of staff had moved in. On the top floor of these new offices Reith organized the construction of a new studio, an artists' waiting area and a small listening-room. The studio was heavily draped with curtains in an attempt to create a completely quiet space. To speak inside this eerie, silent box was said to be 'like hearing a voice disembodied from one's self'. By the end of May the first full-length play had been performed and programmes

Above Between 3 and 12 May 1926 the General Strike meant that the BBC was almost the only means of getting news. As the organization struggled to report disinterestedly on the balance of power between the government and the trades union movement, a police guard protected the entrance to its premises.

Right In 1923 Reith had moved staff into Savoy Place, which was built between 1886 and 1890 as a joint examination hall for the Royal College of Physicians and Surgeons. In 1924 expansion began into the adjacent Savoy Hill (Mansions; pictured), which had previously housed a wide variety of occupants including ale and stout merchants, the National Providence League, architects and solicitors. In 1884 Turkish baths had been licensed in the basement.

were being broadcast simultaneously to the other stations around the country.

The growth in the number of those listening to the radio over the following few years was extraordinary. It was originally thought that about 500,000 people might be interested in listening to the new service, but by 1923 there were already about 200,000 licence holders, and by the end of 1925 more than 1.6 million licences had been sold. A new long-wave transmitter was installed at Daventry, Northamptonshire, in July 1925, and the BBC became fully regionalized, with twenty-one transmitters around the country broadcasting to more than 1.8 million licence holders. These early listeners could, for the very first time, put voices to the faces they had seen in newspapers: their King, the Prince of Wales and their prime minister. It is hard today to imagine the excitement caused by these miraculous voices apparently emanating from the ether. For the first time in history most people in the country were able to set their watches accurately by listening to the Greenwich Time Signal or the chimes of Big Ben. Deciding whether or not to take an umbrella could be done with more confidence, as the BBC became responsible for the weather forecast. (This was read twice: once at natural speed and again, slowly, for long-hand dictation.) People were beginning to rely on the broadcasts in their daily lives.

The first time the real value of the new medium could be seen was during the General Strike of 1926. This was the ideal moment for wireless to show its full potential. The BBC put out five bulletins a day about the changing situation, and listeners were encouraged to help 'spread the news in every possible way'. Although facing criticism that he had been

'too compliant' towards the authorities, Reith managed to maintain the BBC's independence by withstanding the threat of a government takeover, and in so doing won the trust of many listeners. The value of a public broadcasting service independent of political influence could be seen, and on 14 July 1926 it was announced that a new corporation was to be granted the first Royal Charter. Only four years into his job, Reith had ensured that radio had been elevated from an almost purely technological experiment to a service of national importance.

With growing confidence, increasing reliability and royal approval, the BBC became more adventurous in the range and breadth of its service. While Reith had been battling to keep the BBC independent, enthusiastic young engineers had been recording the sounds of an electric eel in a fish tank and a deep-sea diver exploring the River Thames. (Unfortunately for the listeners, he found nothing but beer bottles.) In 1927 other outside broadcast events included the Boat Race, rugby from Twickenham, the FA Cup Final, Wimbledon, the Derby, and cricket from Lord's and the Oval. Less athletic activities included the Ceremony of the Keys (presumably involving much rattling of said keys) as the Tower of London was locked up for the night, along with local entertainment evenings from Eastbourne, Margate and Tunbridge Wells.

Even though the listeners could not actually see the ball, the keys, the newsreaders or the performers, presentation was considered vital. Entertainers were already used to dressing up to perform, and they continued to do so when broadcasting. In January 1926 it was decided that announcers should also wear dinner jackets in the evening. Even the engineers had to

Above, left The early BBC was not a single centralized, London-dominated institution. Transmissions from Manchester and Birmingham were made the day after the first daily broadcast; the Newcastle station was opened on 24 December 1922 and was followed during the next two years by Cardiff, Glasgow, Aberdeen, Bournemouth and Belfast. The approximate range of the early transmitters is indicated on the plan by smaller broken circles, and the wider coverage by the new transmitters is shown by a solid line. The greatest technical achievement of the era was the building in Daventry of Station 5XX, the biggest in the world. By July 1925 it could transmit national programmes across most of England (indicated by the large broken circle).

Above, centre and right The BBC sought to broadcast many different subjects, and the new microphones were placed in a huge array of environments. Early subjects included the voices of King Edward VIII and Winston Churchill, and the sounds of a deep-sea diver exploring the River Thames.

be smart. BBC engineer Robert Wood recalled that 'Reith and Eckersley [the BBC's chief engineer] would have a fit if I turned up in open-necked shirts or Oxford bags'. Apart from looking good, you also had to be careful what you said. An early 'talks' programme by Allen Walker about the Houses of Parliament ended with a casual invitation: 'If any of you would like to be there at ten o'clock tomorrow I will show you round.' The following day 7000 people turned up. The BBC advised greater caution in future.

The BBC handbooks of the late 1920s capture wonderfully the spirit and enthusiasm behind the new medium, and include articles on how programmes were made, reports on artistic and technical progress during the year, advertisements for the latest valves and items on forming 'radio circles' (listening clubs). Listeners were invited to submit plays for broadcast,

or to compose music. Publications and articles in the various BBC handbooks (and, from 1930, yearbooks) provided helpful instruction in 'How to write a Play for the Radio', 'How to Conduct a Wireless Discussion Group', 'How to avoid Electric Shocks' and even 'How to Listen':

Make sure that your set is working properly before you settle down to listen. Choose your programmes as carefully as you choose which theatre to go to. It is just as important to you to enjoy yourself at home as at the theatre. Listen as carefully at home as you do in a theatre or concert hall. You can't get the best out of a programme if your mind is wandering, or if you are playing bridge or reading. Give it your full attention. Try turning out the lights so that your eye is not caught by familiar objects in the room. Your imagination will be twice as vivid. If you only listen with half an ear you haven't a quarter of a right to

WHEATH
ROBINSON

Talks Pamphlets

Every day B.B.C. talks are increasing in popularity. More and more listeners are being attracted to them—a fact which is not very surprising when the quality and importance of these talks is considered, and the authority of the speakers. Practically every series of talks is preceded by the publication of an illustrated and documented pamphlet, which enables listeners to familiarise themselves with the general outline of the subject, and to refer to other sources of information. Full details and rates of subscription may be had of the B.B.C. Bookshop, Savoy Hill, London, W.C.2.

A 2   [9]

*criticize. Think of your favourite occupation. Don't you like a change
sometimes? Give the wireless a rest now and then.*
'Good Listening', from an article in the BBC Yearbook 1930

On 1 January 1927 the BBC became the British Broadcasting
Corporation. Reith had had to take over the adjacent Savoy Hill
building in 1924 to construct more studios to cope with the
demand for programmes. Thirty-one staff had originally moved
to Savoy Place, and now nearly 400 people were packed into
the two buildings. Conditions were cramped and congested,
and there was a desperate need for more space. The BBC's civil
engineer, Marmaduke Tudsbery (1892–1983), was asked to take
'any steps you may consider necessary to bring to our notice
any sites or interesting buildings that you may feel might be
suitable for consideration by the Corporation'.

The BBC's new home would need to be centrally located and
within easy reach of transport facilities. During the following
few months more than twenty sites were considered, most
of them within a short walk of Piccadilly Circus. Tudsbery
diligently recorded a few of the alternatives he had explored,
including the Langham Hotel, the Grand Hotel in Trafalgar
Square, Grosvenor House, Portman Square, the Philharmonic
Hall in Great Portland Street and Bush House, the site that
would eventually be occupied by the BBC's World Service.
However, by the summer of 1927 it was Dorchester House
in Park Lane that stood out. Its grand Palladian style was
impressive, and, having been shown round its large and
elegant rooms, Tudsbery recommended that negotiations
begin for its purchase. It would allow the BBC to send out
another sort of message: the organization was here to stay.

Right Studio Number 1 at Savoy Hill.
The microphone is on a trolley, and
the engineers' cabinet is visible in the
corner of the room. The rapid progress
made during the next ten years in the
design of studios can be seen by
comparing these simple curtain-lined
rooms with the new purpose-built
studios at Broadcasting House (see
pages 51–52).

Below, left Miss Olive Sturgess and
Mr John Huntingdon sing a duet in
the Marconi House studio in 1922.
In the background are the tubular
bells used for the time signals.

Below, right Wireless clubs and radio
circles allowed groups of people to
'listen in' and provided a forum for
discussion of the wide variety of
subjects being broadcast.

THE COCKATOO BROADCASTS
At the London Zoo

Above, left and centre left The bells of Big Ben were first broadcast to usher in 1924. A microphone was placed next to the bell itself, and the chimes were also recorded from afar.

Above, centre right and right Birdsong was a favourite subject for the early broadcasters. On 19 May 1924 the song of a nightingale was broadcast from a wood in Surrey, with cello accompaniment; and a cockatoo got his chance to broadcast to the nation from London Zoo.

Left By the beginning of 1927 there were nearly 400 staff at Savoy Hill, with a similar number in total at stations around the country. As staff numbers continued to grow, the hunt began for a new headquarters. Dorchester House on Park Lane was one of many buildings considered. The BBC eventually decided that the cost of converting an existing building was too high, and Dorchester House was sold in 1929 and demolished to make way for the Dorchester Hotel.

1928

2 February The BBC decides to build new headquarters.
28 February Val Myer's first drawings for the Portland Place site are received by the BBC.
21 November An agreement is signed and exchanged between the BBC and the syndicate to construct Broadcasting House.

1929

25 June The planning application for Broadcasting House is submitted to London County Council.
12 November The BBC Board sets up a Decorations Committee to oversee the design of the studios.

1930

February Basement work on Broadcasting House is complete.
6 October An exhibition is held at 14 Holland Park Road, W14, to give a 'general idea of the type of decorative work suggested for the BBC's new headquarters'.

1931

26 September The BBC begins the move from Savoy Hill to Broadcasting House.

1932

April–May Most BBC staff move from Savoy Hill to Broadcasting House.
1 May Broadcasting House officially opens.
14 May The BBC broadcasts the programme 'Farewell to Savoy Hill' to mark its departure to Broadcasting House.
15 May The first official programme is broadcast from Broadcasting House.

The Building of Broadcasting House

Right An uncredited watercolour shows the awkwardly shaped site that Broadcasting House would occupy. The BBC was willing to lease most of the proposed new building, with the idea that it could sublet any excess space, but by May 1928 Val Myer wrote that the organization 'could scarcely squeeze' into its new home.

Far right Lieutenant-Colonel George Val Myer joined the army at the beginning of the First World War, during which his partner died and his architectural practice failed. For the next three years he stayed in the Disposal Department of the Army, before going to India to become assistant to the Government Architect of Bengal, but after only a year in the post he became ill and had to return to England. He went into partnership with Francis James Watson-Hart (1880–1953) in 1929. The commission for Broadcasting House would test his skills to the limit.

Opposite, left Broadcasting House as it might have been. A perspective drawing of 1928 shows the preferred 'Top Hat design', before site constraints and increasing space requirements forced the building to follow the shape of the site more closely.

Opposite, centre and right Two pre-Broadcasting House buildings by Val Myer in London: Asia House in Lime Street (1912–13; left) and Portsoken House in the Minories (1927–28).

While Tudsbery was busy making plans for the conversion of a suitable building, the freehold of a site on Portland Place was put up for sale. The area had a complex history.

In 1758 Lord Foley had built a large country house for himself on fields where the Langham Hotel now stands. The site had formerly been owned by the Duke of Portland, who had agreed with Foley that the fine views north from his house would be preserved. As the land became more valuable, however, the duke realized that money could be made by developing the surrounding area. A scheme was conjured up to preserve Foley's views while allowing the duke to profit, and Portland Place was constructed by building new houses either side of a 100-foot-wide (30 m) clear strip of land running north from Foley's house. To the east of Portland Place was the house and garden of 1 Foley Place (which took its name from its neighbour to the south-west), built in 1783 by the architect James Wyatt (1746–1813).

Foley's mansion was demolished to make way for a house for Sir James Langham, designed between 1813 and 1815 by John Nash (1752–1835). Nash was also working on a plan to extend the wide avenue of Portland Place south, down to St James's Park. His designs upset Langham, however, and Nash was forced to re-route his avenue around Langham's property. Making the best of this adversity, Nash created the distinctive porch of All Souls Church (1822–25) to resemble a circular temple. According to the architect and planner Steen Eiler Rasmussen, his design effortlessly connected Regent Street and Portland Place 'like the knee of a jointed doll'.

This simple description of historical events (see maps on page 24) explains the oddly shaped site that Broadcasting

House would eventually occupy. In 1927 Wyatt's house stood to the north of All Souls Church and to the north-east of the Langham Hotel, which had replaced Langham's house. In this year a syndicate of speculators employed forty-four-year-old architect Lieutenant-Colonel George Val Myer to produce a drawing showing smart flats or a hotel, as an 'indication that the site and architect were capable of a striking building'.

Trim, thoughtful and slightly saturnine in appearance, Val Myer (1883–1959) had been articled to John Belcher in 1900 and started his own practice aged just nineteen. By 1906 he was in partnership with J.W. Fair, and he went on to design Asia House in Lime Street, London (1912–13; opposite, centre). By the time of his application for fellowship of the Royal Institute of British Architects (RIBA) in January 1929 he had completed a large number of medium-sized houses all over England (especially in the south), business premises and factory buildings. In 1927 he was completing Portsoken House (1927–28; opposite, right), which, according to RIBA records, was 'a large block of offices and shops in a restrained and modern manner'. The building he sketched for the syndicate was shaped like a top hat, its upper floors fashionably set back in the spirit of an American skyscraper. The site would eventually provide Val Myer with the commission of a lifetime, but many difficulties lay ahead of him.

The syndicate decided that identifying a client would be financially less risky than a speculative venture, and by February 1928 Tudsbery had been informed that it would be prepared to erect a building for the BBC. The syndicate, represented by Robert Solomon, instructed Val Myer to 'put before the BBC a perspective drawing and sketch plans for a

building designed especially for the BBC's needs'. Shortly afterwards Val Myer received a letter from Tudsbery, explaining that a BBC Governors' meeting on Wednesday 14 March would decide the fate of the site, and intimating the likely outcome: 'your clients will then receive an official intimation from our Director-General'.

After nearly a year of looking for a suitable building to convert, and aware of the mounting complexity and cost of reconfiguring an existing property, the Governors were probably beginning to realize that a new building might be an attractive option after all. By the end of the 1920s such purpose-built broadcast centres as the Haus des Rundfunks in Berlin (1929–30), the multi-purpose Radio City development in New York (1929–32) and the Dutch Labour Party Broadcasting Station at Hilversum (1932) were being planned overseas and beginning to hint at a new architecture of broadcasting.

The Portland Place location was attractive, as the BBC could use the nearby Queen's Hall for performances. It was decided that Val Myer should continue to work on a design with Tudsbery, and the syndicate was instructed to ask Val Myer to prepare some preliminary plans to enable the Governors to 'see how far his sketches would suit the Corporation's detailed requirements'. The BBC needed 60,000 square feet (5600 sq. m) of office space, with a further 40,000 square feet (3700 sq. m) for possible future expansion. The BBC did not imagine that it would need the whole building, and Tudsbery was instructed not to proceed with the project unless he was able to sublet some of the space. In reply to the BBC's invitation, the syndicate's agents, Montagu's and Cox & Cardale, wrote to the Corporation's Assistant Director-General, stating that their clients 'had always felt that this was a unique site, worthy of housing a national institution instead of being put to a more mundane use, such as the development of flats', and that they were 'accordingly much gratified at your suggestion that plans should be prepared for the accommodation of the British Broadcasting Corporation'. A few weeks later Val Myer proposed starting the project on 24 June 1928. He suggested that the building work could start as early as September, and could be completed by March 1930. He estimated that £260,000 would be required to finance the construction of the building, and the cost for the whole project was expected to be around £390,000.

The joint report

Tudsbery and Val Myer presented their ideas for the site in a joint report signed and dated 3 July 1928. It confidently stated: 'The building, as planned, will give all the accommodation required for the present needs of the Corporation besides leaving a reserve of more than twenty thousand [square] feet [1800 sq. m] of excellent office space on the first and second floors, which, together with the shops and bank on the ground and sub-ground floors (amounting to 14,425 [square] ft [1300 sq. m]), it is proposed to let off to other tenants.'

In order to find the required floor space, their proposal squeezed as much as possible out of the narrow and awkwardly shaped piece of land. Their drawings showed a building that pushed as far as possible to the edges of the site, was as high as permitted and went as far down into the ground as was practical. There were to be three basement floors and eight

floors above street level. Val Myer and Tudsbery proposed a radical solution for the design of the new studios. They decided to place them all in an eleven-storey tower in the middle of the building and wrap the office space around it. This would mean that although the studios would have no natural light or ventilation, they would be protected by the offices from the traffic noise of Portland Place. Val Myer later explained their thinking:

The guiding principle was to exploit to the utmost the peculiar advantages in shape and size of the offices and similar departments to which daylight is essential … . On the other hand, the studios and their suites, for which insulation from external noise is the first need, have been grouped in a vast central tower of heavy brickwork, ventilated by artificial means and protected from the streets by the complete outer layer of offices.

Parts of the ground and basement floors were to be sublet for shops, and a bank was to be located on the corner of the building facing south down Regent Street. The building would have no fewer than five entrances: one for the bank, one for shop tenants, two for the BBC (one for staff and one for artists) and one for goods. The BBC's reception area was to be on the Langham Street side of the building, with six studios and a 'super-studio' or concert hall of 5000 square feet (460 sq. m), 'capable of seating a thousand people', at the top of the building. A car lift would provide access to the three basement floors. Thirty-six vehicles could be parked there, with an extraordinary, novel proposal for a small 'railway' to move cars to the parking spaces. It was an innovative and

Below Val Myer's intention was to vary the building line to allow a symmetrical, semicircular elevation facing Regent Street. This would have created more public space between Broadcasting House and All Souls Church, and widened Langham Street.

Below, centre The history of the immediate area resulted in the oddly shaped peninsula of land that would prove so difficult for Val Myer to work with. Diagrams of the area in (from top) 1791, 1832 and 1932.

Below, right The section drawing from the joint report shows the cut-backs on the upper floors necessary to maintain the rights of light to the buildings to the east of the adjoining Langham Street. The studios in the centre of the building are interspersed with other uses to avoid sound leaking out between rooms.

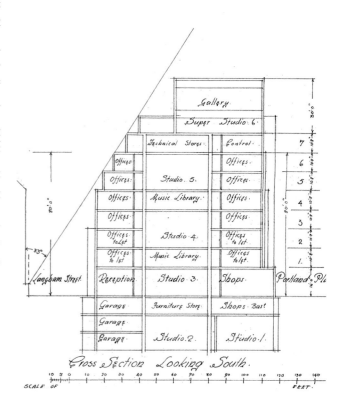

daring design. On 21 November 1928 the BBC and the syndicate signed an agreement to develop the design further. It required the syndicate to proceed at their own cost, to the 'approval and satisfaction' of Tudsbery. However, this would prove to be far from easy to achieve.

On 27 November 1928 the BBC issued a press release that reflected their architect's vision for the building. It stated: 'The design of the building will be simple, almost severe, depending for its effect more on the grouping of masonry masses than upon profusion of detail.' Val Myer had been forced early on to compromise his original vision for a completely symmetrical building. The joint-report design showed the top floor pushed westwards and the upper floors on the Langham Street side of the building cut back to preserve light to the houses to the east of the site.

Although the BBC would owe much to their amiable and productive partnership, there were other problems for Val Myer and Tudsbery to resolve as they worked closely together over the following months. The practicalities of getting a full orchestra and 1000 people up to the roof of the building (as well as sorting out all the necessary entrances and fire exits) were too difficult for Val Myer to surmount. A few weeks into the design process Tudsbery was forced to write to Reith, saying that the original idea of placing the 'Great Hall' (concert hall) at the top of the building was being dropped in favour of locating it on the lower ground floor. 'As a result it was necessary to re-design the elevation above the 80 foot [24 m] level … a feature of the original perspective that I understand you don't altogether care for.'

Val Myer wanted his building to have a symmetrical elevation facing Regent Street, but that particular part of the site was an awkward shape. He decided that the solution was to build on part of Portland Place, to create a more generous end to his building, and give some land back at the junction of Portland Place and Regent Street. His stated intention was for 'a symmetrical and dignified building' (as 'so important and commanding a position' at the top of Regent Street deserved), and he did not consider that he needed to 'enlarge upon the advantages of the open space suggested at the junction of Langham Street, All Souls Place and Langham Place'. Meetings were held with Marylebone Borough Council and London County Council to discuss his proposition, and a new building line was agreed on 14 January 1929. Recalling events years later, Tudsbery claimed the credit for 'resisting the highways pressure for an easement with resulting disastrous loss of space, and so saving the entire project from disaster'.

All Souls Church

During the debate about the line of the building, there had been discussions about the possibility of removing the steps from the church to help to ease the traffic problem. The minutes of a meeting held by the London County Council Building Act Committee in January 1929 recorded:

We have told you we propose to negotiate to take off the steps of this church and eventually – it will be rather difficult to arrange – we may be able to get this whole tower removed altogether which will make a

Below The ground-floor plan in the joint report shows the strategy for planning the building. Unusually for a building with such a deep plan, all the space is used, even without any fresh air or light being provided to its centre. Note the initial idea for the semicircular banking hall at the prow of the building, and the curved bay of shops proposed on the ground floor. A clause in the lease declared that certain trades were prohibited on the site, including those of 'a butcher … slaughterman, fishmonger, tallow chandler melter … tripe boiler … tavern keeper … railway parcel booking office carrier, quasi-medical or quasi-surgical establishment, brothel or bagnio keeper'.

Overleaf As the scheme developed the elevation on Portland Place had to be modified, as can be seen in a perspective view by George Farey. Note the publicly accessible ground floor and the terrace and veranda at the top of the building. The final design for the ground floor was rather less welcoming.

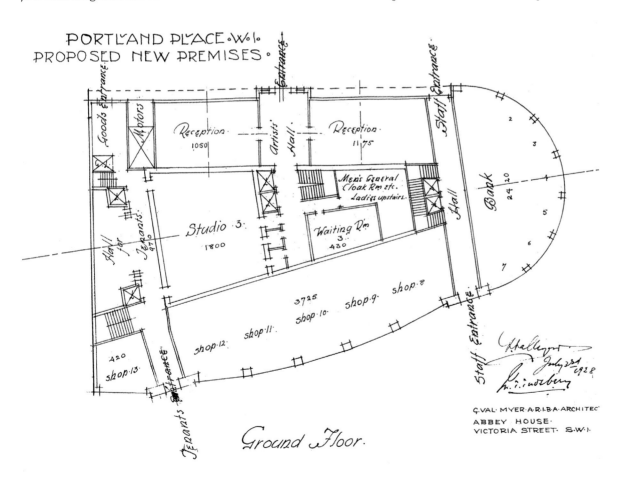

PORTLAND PLACE · W.1.
PROPOSED NEW PREMISES.

Ground Floor.

G· VAL· MYER· A· R· I· B· A· ARCHITECT
ABBEY HOUSE
VICTORIA STREET· S· W· 1.

very good thoroughfare right the way through. Our idea at the moment is to get these steps at least taken off and to cut steps inside the porch to give an approach there. That scheme was approved by the Church authorities some years ago. It only fell through on account of expense. They wanted compensation which we didn't see our way to give them[;] now we might have to.

A month later, sensing that a new opportunity was about to present itself, Robert Solomon wrote directly to Reith: 'I think you will be interested to hear that All Souls Church, Portland Place, is about to be scheduled as redundant …. I have an appointment this Friday with the surveyors concerned. Please treat this information as confidential.' A few days later he wrote again:

I have just returned from an informal interview with Mr Marr Johnson of Messrs Cluttons, who will have disposal of this church if and when an order is made for its sale. No doubt the portico and steps will be acquired by the authorities for street widening purposes. This will leave a square site with a ground area of approximately 8000 square feet [740 sq. m] (perhaps a little more) which would lend itself admirably for the purpose of a concert hall. Would the BBC be interested in the site?

Reith responded warmly:

Many thanks for your note of yesterday. The proposition is very interesting … the situation is that we are forming a permanent orchestra, in conjunction with Sir Thomas Beecham, as you probably know; the prices for the Queen's Hall are exorbitant, and there are periodic rumours that it is to be turned into a cinema or something of that sort; we are likely to arrange the orchestra on a tentative basis in the autumn of this year …. The above is all confidential, but I thought I should let you know, and I am sure you will be interested.

But despite the entrepreneurial efforts of Solomon and the 'exorbitant' prices of the Queen's Hall, the proposal to demolish All Souls Church appears to stop there. There is no further correspondence on file, and it seems that Nash's church had a lucky escape. An original offer of £50 was made by the syndicate to church funds; it was increased to £75 for subsequent damage and loss of light, and to allow for the re-glazing of the church's windows.

'Out of harmony'?

Given the importance of the project, Val Myer and Tudsbery agreed that some support from the press would be advantageous. Articles appeared in the *Wireless Magazine* in February 1929 and the *Daily Mail* on 6 June 1929, headlined 'Full Use of the Site'. They described how the scheme for the BBC differed from the 'top hat' scheme, and made 'more practical use' of the space the land allowed. In the meantime, Val Myer had managed to squeeze some more space out of the Portland Place side of the building by making the upper floors of the building curved, to follow the new line of the street. A perspective drawing (pictured right), reproduced in the *BBC Yearbook 1930*, shows the more familiar elevation we see today. Val Myer explained in the *BBC Yearbook 1932*: 'At an early date … I realized that the site possessed a rare virtue in the long curve of the Western side, and so, in organizing the proportion of my masses and the play of light and shade,

I tried to make full use of the gracious horizontal lines which this curve suggested.'

Not everybody appreciated Val Myer's efforts, and there were some serious concerns about the plain look of the building. On 22 April 1929 Edward Blount, acting for another nearby landowner, examined Val Myer's drawings. 'Without in any way criticizing the architectural treatment', he wrote (although he went on to do just that), he thought 'that the elevation of the building as designed will be so much out of harmony with anything in the neighbourhood that I am not able to give the drawing my approval …. I consider that portions of the estate belonging to my clients, the Howard de Walden estate and the Audley Trust, will be seriously damaged.' Three days later, he went so far as to suggest that the prepared elevation should be submitted to the President of the RIBA for 'an opinion as to its architectural merits, having regard to the position of the building, its immediate surroundings and the future development of Portland Place'. Word got back to Reith pretty quickly, and he wrote to Val Myer on the same day, rather ominously requesting that he should meet the Governors for the first time, so that 'there may be a general interchange of opinions on architectural embellishments and things of that order'.

Reith had been concerned for some time that the building should have a less 'institutional' look about it, and asked if something could be done to break up 'the plain front'. Tudsbery, for his part, disliked the small windows, which seemed old-fashioned to him and would be difficult to keep clean. Nevertheless, Val Myer held on to his architectural ideals, and was equally dogged about the idea of a large studio at the top of the building: not the 'super-studio' originally proposed, but substantial nonetheless. He responded to the criticisms in a letter of some charm, defending his choice of fenestration and extolling the virtues of the windows' small panes and vertical proportions.

Val Myer also had to deal with the constant increase in the amount of studio and office space required by Reith's growing organization. As early as May 1928, Val Myer had visualized that the Corporation could move to a building into which it could expand; the BBC 'now had to contemplate a building into which they could scarcely squeeze'. The idea of the bank had been quickly dropped, but now the basement car park with its radical railway was removed to make more space.

The pace of accommodating these changes must have been frenetic. Despite the problems, and less than a year from the joint-report scheme, the drawings were sufficiently advanced to be submitted to London County Council on 25 June 1929. The scheme had suffered, however. After all the work, Tudsbery had to confess that the revised designs were 'second best' and not as convincing as his and Val Myer's joint-report proposal.

Building Broadcasting House
Once the syndicate had acquired the site in 1928, Wyatt's house was demolished and foundation work quickly started. At nearly 40 feet (12 m) below pavement level, the building would need one of London's deepest basements. Some 43,000 tons of sticky and waterlogged clay were excavated, a sewer was encased in concrete, and a 600-foot-deep (180 m) borehole sunk to supply water for the building. The basement work was complete by February 1930, and by the early spring,

bricklayers were using engineering bricks to build the 4-foot 6-inch-thick (1.4 m) walls around the outside of the studio tower.

The frame of the building rose steadily out of the ground. Some of the largest steel members ever used in Britain were being hoisted into place, using a new type of crane. A watercolour shows that the steel frame was complete up to the second floor in July 1930; by October 1930 it had reached the fourth floor, and the large sloping roof was beginning to take shape. While the outside walls were clad in smooth Portland stone, thin reinforced-concrete floors were laid inside the building, and the studio walls were filled with eel grass to provide acoustic insulation. However, efforts to create the world's quietest broadcast building were turning out to be rather noisy. With 400 men working on the construction site, the Marchioness of Winchester, a local resident, complained in a letter published in the *Daily Express* that 'thousands of people in the neighbourhood of Portland Place are deprived of sleep all night' because of 'the unceasing and excruciating noise caused by the work on the new BBC headquarters'.

Although no foundation stone had been laid, it was decided to create a time capsule in a steel box to be buried within the building. In July 1930 a box size was agreed with Val Myer, but then Tudsbery changed his mind and decided that he did not want to fold the foolscap documents that were to be placed inside the capsule. He also commented that the original size was 'somewhat small for all the junk that we propose to deposit in it'. On 21 July 1930 a deflated Val Myer wrote to Tudsbery about the box, also expressing his feelings about all the other changes that had been made to his design. He stated revealingly: 'I have looked through these plans again with great interest and a certain degree of disappointment as I find that the scheme shown compares so very unfavourably with that which is now so rapidly taking shape for the Corporation's new home.' Tudsbery replied with some sympathy: 'As you say, the original scheme compares very unfavourably… but instead of feeling it a matter for disappointment, I am somewhat elated to think [that] our two years of hard labour since the joint report plans were prepared have obviously been spent to very good purpose!'

As Tudsbery commiserated with Val Myer, an exhibition was opened on 6 October 1930 at 14 Holland Park Road, London, to give a 'general idea of the type of decorative work suggested for the BBC's new headquarters'. Eric Gill (1882–1940) had been commissioned by the BBC in October 1929, via the art critic Herbert Read, to produce sculpture for Broadcasting House. The exhibition featured a model of the new concert hall and provided the first glimpse of Gill's designs, which would be vitally important to the success of the building.

The studios
Although the office spaces inside the new building would need, in Val Myer's words, 'endless flexibility for sub-division', their design would be relatively straightforward. However, the studios inside Val Myer's tower required much more careful consideration. As the design had developed, it had become clear that more studios would be needed than originally envisaged. It emerged that the rehearsal time for a programme was often more than three times longer than the live performance, and some types of programme, such as a

AN ARTIST'S PENCIL NOTES ON WORK IN PROGRESS
(Mr. Gill in the top left-hand corner.)

Above and right The construction of Broadcasting House was carefully recorded. The photograph shows the steel frame within the walls and the outer Portland stone cladding in October 1930. The site hoarding has an advertisement for *The Big House* (a film from the same year about a convict who falls in love with his new cellmate's sister, only to become embroiled in a planned break-out certain to have lethal consequences). 'Big House' was also used to describe Broadcasting House at the time.

Opposite, top left The vast slate roof nears completion. It was hidden from Regent Street by a parapet wall, which gave the illusion from that direction of a symmetrical building.

Opposite, top right The steel frame is erected at basement level. Great efforts were made to avoid sound transference through the steel structure between studios and offices. The building used some of the largest steel members in the country, fabricated by the contractors Moreland Hayne and Company. The stanchions rest on solid steel blooms weighing 7 tons each.

Opposite, bottom left The walls of the studio tower, 4 feet 6 inches (1.4 m) wide at their bases, were made entirely out of blue Staffordshire bricks to cope with the enormous weight of the structure. More than 2,630,000 bricks were used, and about 400 men worked on the site at any one time.

Opposite, bottom right Excavation work began early in 1929 and was completed in February 1930 at a depth of 45 feet (13.7 m). A borehole 7¼ inches (18.4 cm) wide and 600 feet (180 m) deep was sunk to supply fresh drinking water; it was never used, since the Metropolitan Water Board was able to supply water on acceptable terms.

Above The small exhibition at
14 Holland Park Road in October
1930 showed the various ideas for
the decoration of the building. Eric
Gill was commissioned by the BBC
in October 1929 to produce a series
of sculptures for the new building.

Opposite, top Raymond McGrath's
sketch for the vaudeville studio in the
basement. A balcony provided more
space for an audience, and helped to
create atmosphere for the broadcast.

Opposite, bottom left The decoration
of studio number 9 at Savoy Hill tried
to make the dark, windowless space a
little more inspiring.

Opposite, bottom right McGrath's
worm's-eye-view painting shows the
bright colours and smooth lines of
the vaudeville studio.

'dramatic play', could require as many as six studios at once.
Studios of different sizes were needed to contain the varied
departments and create different acoustics. The joint-report
scheme contained six studios. The new plan was to squeeze
twenty-two into the studio tower.

It was apparent to Reith that spending hour upon hour
in stuffy spaces with no natural light would depress his
staff. Early performers had referred to the windowless boxes
at Savoy Hill as 'the Black Hole of Calcutta', and attempts
had been made there to liven up some of the newer studios
by doing away with the dusty old drapes and decorating
the walls with felt-backed wallpaper to provide some degree
of acoustic absorption. In November 1929 responsibility for
overseeing the design of the new studios in Broadcasting
House was given to the Assistant Controller, Commander
V.H. Goldsmith, who was made chairman of the newly
formed Studio Decoration Committee. Also on the
committee was Dr Montague Rendall, described as
'the representative of the Governors and the ultimate
authority in matters of decoration at Broadcasting House'.
After some debate, the committee agreed that a number
of designers would be needed to provide some variety,
although 'not so many as to make things unmanageable'.
Goldsmith warned that unless the appearance of the new
studios was carefully designed and monitored, even 'a
harmonious studio soon has the knick-knack appearance
of a secondhand shop'. The creation of twenty-two brand-
new studios was a magnificent opportunity. As Goldsmith
would later explain, each individual studio would become
a unique work of art:

*It was an opportunity of modern decorative design on a more extensive
scale than is common, and was perhaps[,] up to this moment, the
greatest opportunity in this country. It was felt that as a public
institution the Corporation must bring the same courage of outlook
to its employment of the visual arts as it endeavours to bring to its
utilization of the arts of speech and music. The latest discoveries in
new materials and their application must be explored.*

Tudsbery and his technical decoration sub-committee
would oversee the functional requirements of the studios.
The twenty-two spaces would be divided into groups,
roughly floor by floor, and various designers allocated
accordingly. The committee entrusted Val Myer with the
decoration of the large concert and entrance halls. To carry
out most of the remaining work, they found three young
architects – Raymond McGrath, Serge Chermayeff and
Wells Coates – who would later be referred to as the 'Three
Musketeers' by the editor of the influential journal the
Architectural Review, Hubert de Cronin Hastings.

Raymond McGrath (1903–1977) was given the job of
co-ordinating the interior design. He was Australian and, at
twenty-six, the youngest of the three. He had just completed
a series of extraordinarily poetic interiors at a house in
Cambridge. 'Finella' had a bathroom with aluminium walls,
copper doors, rubber floors and mirrored ceilings. Serge
Chermayeff (1900–1996), born in Groznyy, Chechnia, was
twenty-nine and a champion ballroom dancer. He had
captured attention a few years earlier with his interior for
the Cambridge Theatre in London, an immensely stylish
space that was said to be 'an exhibit in itself'. Finally,

Wells Coates (1895–1958), a thirty-four-year-old Canadian with a doctorate in engineering, was given some of the more technical spaces to design.

The committee decided that the studios should be designed as suites of rooms on each floor, each with its own waiting-room. In addition to the work of the 'Three Musketeers', two 'one-off' studios on the third floor were given to Edward Maufe, who was asked to design the religious studio (presumably because of his previous experience of churches), and a single 'talks' studio was commissioned from Dorothy Warren Trotter.

The design of the new studios would be immensely challenging. It was reported in the *Architectural Review* of August 1932 that 'the required level of silence necessary for Broadcasting is seven decibels above the level of hearing; the equivalent of the sound created by the rustling of leaves set up by a gentle breeze in, say, a perfectly quiet spot on a summer's night'. The *BBC Handbook 1929* had confidently stated that 'the technical design constants of the studio given a shape, size and material were more or less calculable', but in truth it was far from being an exact science. Although the BBC had had some experience of designing studios, there was little established acoustic precedent on which to draw.

Apart from the lack of data, there was one big problem facing the designers: finding the high-quality British materials that could satisfy strict acoustic requirements. In the second half of 1931, the economic depression and subsequent trade tariffs meant that the use of foreign materials was prohibited. The designers, therefore, had to 'buy British', or at least buy

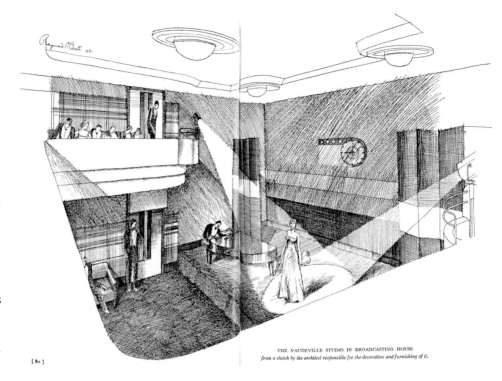

[80]

THE VAUDEVILLE STUDIO IN BROADCASTING HOUSE
from a sketch by the architect responsible for the decoration and furnishing of it.

33

Above Strict acoustic requirements meant that the materials used in the studios had to be carefully chosen to avoid unwanted acoustic reflection. Picture frames were not allowed to contain glass. As the BBC began broadcasting from the top-floor studio, the basement studios were still being completed, as can be seen in these images from March 1932. The walls were covered in various materials, including Lincrusta (left; centre left) and shiny acoustic panels (centre right). Eel grass was used as sound insulation within the walls (far right).

Opposite Reith symbolically locks the west door of Savoy Hill for the last time. Today the round edge of the plaque reading 'BBC' can still be seen on the wall by the steps of the building, but the lettering has been removed.

from the British colonies. Although much of the raw timber for the panelling and office furniture came from within the empire, there was great difficulty in obtaining British substitutes for all the materials needed in the studios. McGrath had originally wanted a cellulose sheet from Germany called Trolit for the studio walls, and was forced to write to thirty firms in an attempt to find a suitable substitute. Goldsmith later remarked on how difficult it was to get British firms to try different ideas during the construction of Broadcasting House.

The technical problems involved in designing the studios fascinated the young designers. They saw the design of radio studios as a 'modern' problem, and essentially a functional, not a decorative, challenge. It fitted well the growing idea that good modern design should be functional and efficient. Importantly, it also allowed them to distance their modern schemes from the more traditional, decorative interior design of the period. The designers were particularly taken with the 'raw' appearance of the available acoustic materials, and four types of building board were eventually used in the studios. Donnacona, made in Canada from spruce fibre, was a buff-coloured wall board with a rough texture. Likewise, Beatl, a substitute for the unavailable Trolit, was a sound-absorbent laminated sheet with a surface impervious to water, and could be worked like timber. With a paper backing it could even be used as a wall covering. On occasion, as at Savoy Hill, felt and wallpaper were also used. The idea was then to attach the various materials with battens on to plastered walls to create different degrees of sound absorbency, from resonant timber to absorbent insulation.

On the floors were rugs patterned with abstract designs in vibrant colours. They were useful and beautiful but, importantly, also fun. The few manufacturers who were persuaded to set up machines to produce new papers, synthetic materials and specially woven fabrics later added these items to their own ranges as standard products. The results of their labours would be extraordinary.

Moving in

As the building neared completion the press followed progress closely, and various articles appeared over the next few months. The *Daily Express* carried the headline: 'New £500,000 Home of Wireless' and described the building as the 'brain centre of modern civilization' and the 'world's new voice', while asking the question: 'Will it become the most

potent educational factor since Caxton first introduced his printing press into England?' The *Evening Standard* of 30 December 1931 announced, even more dramatically: 'New Wonder Home of the BBC'.

In September 1931 some of the administrative, technical and publishing staff had begun to move into the new building. Given the size of the organization, the *BBC Yearbook 1932* stated: 'A gradual transfer is inevitable[;] this makes it impossible for Broadcasting House to have an official opening on a given date, and the BBC has therefore decided against any form of opening ceremony.' As the staff moved in, the row of shops on Portland Place was left unfinished and boarded up, the basement studios were still being completed, and Gill's sculpture for the niche above the entrance was conspicuously absent. However, aerials had been erected on the roof and the building tested throughout the winter and early spring to ensure that it was ready for transmitting programmes. On 15 March 1932 the first musical programme featured the popular Henry Hall and his BBC Dance Orchestra. Henry took the microphone and introduced himself to the world: 'Hello everyone, this is Henry Hall speaking', whereupon his signature tune struck up: 'It's just the time for dancing'. Three days later the first regular news bulletin was read out. With the tests successfully completed, the rest of the BBC and the programme-makers could move in. The 'big move' took place over four weekends in April 1932 and needed 160 van loads to move 300 tons of equipment, files and books. It was proudly reported that not one single breakage had occurred or piece of paper been lost.

Reith can be seen in photographs symbolically locking the doors at Savoy Hill for the very last time (opposite). The old broadcasting world had been left behind for ever. A BBC yearbook article of 1932 entitled 'Goodbye to Savoy Hill' nostalgically announced that 'however splendid the new headquarters, the BBC will always remember its years at Savoy Hill with pride and affection, as the home in which it spent its childhood and grew up to man's estate'.

For a building of the scale and technical ambition of Broadcasting House to be completed and operational in less than three-and-a-half years was a remarkable achievement. Less than ten years on from its small, experimental beginnings, the BBC had its own state-of-the-art headquarters and was about to embark on what would become an extraordinary period in broadcasting history. Broadcasting House was ready to speak to the world.

1932

7 July King George V and Queen Mary officially open Broadcasting House.

22 August The first experimental television broadcast from Broadcasting House.

19 December The Empire Service (precursor of the World Service) is launched from Broadcasting House.

25 December King George V becomes the first monarch to deliver a Christmas Day message by radio.

1933

February Initial plans are made for a new extension to Broadcasting House.

16 June First broadcast programme of the BBC organ from the concert hall.

28 July The first female BBC radio announcer (Sheila Barrett) broadcasts from the new building.

1934

The film *Death at Broadcasting House* is released.

Broadcasting House in the 1930s

Top The cover of the *BBC Yearbook 1930*.

Above There were four flagstaffs on the building. This flag symbolizes the BBC's aspiration to broadcast to the world.

Above, right Broadcasting House stood out amongst central London's soot-stained architecture. The Queen's Hall, seen to the right of All Souls Church, was destroyed by a bomb on 10 May 1941.

Opposite Eric Gill's head of Prospero is finally installed over the main entrance.

Inspire all those who will speak, or sing or play, with noble ideals that they may give of their best, whether grave or gay, instructive or humorous, and men may feel it is filling a real purpose in life for the common good.
Reverend Pat McCormick of St Martin-in-the-Fields, at the very first morning service in Broadcasting House

Reaction to the 'New Tower of London'
Val Myer's new building was certainly distinctive. In the spring of 1932 it stood white and gleaming, towering above the surrounding soot-stained Georgian and Edwardian architecture. To the casual observer there could be no doubt of its purpose. The various clues as to the identity of the new leaseholder included the three radio masts on the roof and a new BBC coat of arms, sculpted by E. Armonier to a design by

Val Myer. To top things off, a specially designed flag showed a terrestrial globe surrounded by the seven other planets known at the time. Ariel, from Shakespeare's *The Tempest*, had been chosen by the BBC Governors as an appropriate metaphor for the new magic of broadcasting. Gill was still busy completing his main work for the building, a giant Prospero (who symbolized wisdom and benevolence) sending a naked Ariel out into the world. However, his other pieces of sculpture had been finished. Above the concert hall entrance, Ariel was positioned between Wisdom and Gaiety; over the large reception window he could hear 'celestial music'; and above the artists' entrance he is seen again, 'piping to the children'. Smaller motifs on the outside of the building included a repeating wave design and 'birds of the air'. A photograph of the building on the cover of the *BBC Yearbook 1930* sends

out a very clear message: the BBC would be broadcasting to the world from this building.

The austere-looking building seemed to have one foot in the past and another in the future. It bore a family resemblance to a new generation of modern-classical buildings springing up in London at the time, such as Broadway House (1929), Shell-Mex House (1931), Brettenham House and Senate House (both 1932). These buildings had inherited a DNA that was certainly classical, but with only a trace of a decorative gene. Long rows of traditional, vertically proportioned windows in Broadcasting House seemed to emphasize the curve of the front of the new building and the shallow depressions and deep lines cut into the pure and clean monolithic stone surface of the building by way of decoration. This meant that Broadcasting House was not a place for shadows to linger. Professor Charles Reilly, a 'modern classicist' and the respected Head of the School of Architecture in Liverpool, writing in the *BBC Yearbook* 1933, was understandably sympathetic to Val Myer's cause. He thought it was right that the building make some concessions to its context, and that the windows provided 'a contrasting texture to the stone, and were in sympathy with the surrounding buildings'. After all, 'the most we could expect given the historic nature of the area was a certain "neighbourliness", which will make the building consort fairly well with both its present neighbours and its new ones when they arise'.

Nautical references to Broadcasting House abounded in the national press. The curved and streamlined shape of the building, with its flags, masts and 'port-holes' in the top-floor studio, allowed easy comparisons with the bow of a ship. Others extended the nautical analogy to criticize the design. One critic described it as a 'petrified dreadnought', and another as an 'overloaded aircraft carrier', because of its vast sloping roof to one side. *The Listener* magazine described it as a 'leviathan of a building' and suggested that 'not the dove or the eagle, but the white elephant should be its crest'. In typically direct fashion, the architectural historian Nikolaus Pevsner simply called it 'an ugly duckling'.

Yet to others Broadcasting House was just not modern enough. In *An Introduction to Modern Architecture*, written in 1940, J.M. Richards complained that 'the compromise of leaving off the period architecture but retaining the academic formulae by no means produces modern architecture. It only produces crude massive buildings like Shell-Mex House, London, or Broadcasting House[,] that are superficially imposing, but possess neither the aesthetic of a real modern building nor the subtlety of the honest period piece. They are examples of what happens when architecture tries to be "safe".'

The 1920s and 1930s were a highly complex period in British architectural history, and Broadcasting House seemed to capture perfectly at least part of the heated debate about which direction the architecture of the time should take. Many of the architectural critics' opinions about the external appearance of the newly completed building depended on whether they were modernist or traditionalist. Some were both. Reilly wrote that 'Val Myer has certainly managed to give his building a different air from that of the ordinary office block, and to suggest that it serves some new purpose.' As a

Opposite The nearly completed building in a photograph dated June 1932 (still awaiting the installation of Eric Gill's sculpture of Prospero and Ariel). The cost of the new building was £500,000 (around £26.2 million in 2006 prices). Window-boxes on the third, fifth and eighth floors provided a splash of colour against the austere façade, filled with daffodils, geraniums or chrysanthemums according to the season.

Below The completed west elevation. A comparison with the perspective on pages 26–27 shows that the curving top floor behind the clock was never constructed.

Below, right Three other large 'Houses' of the period: Shell-Mex House (top) by Ernest Joseph, Brettenham House (centre) by W. & E. Hunt and Senate House (bottom) by Charles Holden.

champion of modern design, the *Architectural Review* dedicated a special issue of its journal to the new building in August 1932. It was at best lukewarm to the external 'stripped classical' appearance of the building. In an article entitled 'The New Tower of London', it stated that the building represented 'a struggle between moribund traditionalism and inventive modernism' and that 'the Langham Hotel is faced with a more prepossessing monster, whose points, although not of the first order, make a certain show and contribution to London's gaiety'. The journal went on to suggest that, to the impartial viewer at least, it might be 'called a failure as an aesthetic entity, a confused agglomeration of good and bad ideas uncoordinated or unredeemed by a single mind or certain taste', but pointed out fairly that this was to ignore some of the compromises Val Myer had been forced to make, or, as the *Architectural Review* coyly called them, these 'eternal English circumstances'.

Val Myer responded badly to the early criticism. In a letter to *The Builder*, published in June 1932, he lashed out at the critics:

The great difficulty in the way of art criticism of any kind is the fact that the majority of critics owe their existence, as such, rather to their literary or journalistic gifts than to their knowledge or taste in the art upon which they give opinions …. With regard to professional critics, their livelihood depends upon their market value, and that, unfortunately, bears a much closer relationship to the originality of their viewpoint than to the soundness of their criticisms … generally speaking, I think it is better to say nothing if one cannot say nice things.

The *Architectural Review* suggested that the major problem with Broadcasting House was not the building itself, but the choice of site. The 'exigencies of the site, its peculiar shape', which was described as being like a 'lopsided potato or sausage balloon', were seen as having appeared to prevent Val Myer from exploiting the 'full possibilities of the plan … why this particular site was chosen, is not for us to enquire, but it has certainly proved a hard task for the architect'. Reilly also finished his forthright article in the *BBC Yearbook 1933* by questioning the BBC's decision to build on Portland Place, but concluded that Val Myer had made the best of a difficult job: 'In an age of transition on a difficult and restricted site, and with the most interesting things in his building necessarily hidden, one can congratulate the architect on a very notable achievement. One is a little less certain about congratulating the BBC who set him the problem.'

Robert Byron concluded the introduction to his review of the building in the *Architectural Review* with his own views on Val Myer's letter: '

Lt.-Colonel Val Myer's building is being paid for with public money, and it is public money that has made his name as an architect. I will attempt no analysis of the building, gentle or otherwise. But speaking not as a professional critic prostituting himself for the meagre husks thrown by the Architectural Review, but as a former licence holder, I would beg Lt.-Colonel Val Myer not to suppose that he is doomed henceforth to comfortable oblivion. If he chooses to set himself up as an avowed enemy not only of critics, but of all of those people who are concerned for the appearance of our streets … the challenge will be accepted.'

Inside Broadcasting House

A worthy edifice, fitted to house the marvels it contains.
Film, BBC: *The Voice of Britain*, 1934

The royal opening of Broadcasting House by King George V took place on 7 July 1932. Most records agree that the building was officially opened on 1 May that year, and by the following day it was, quite literally, fully occupied. Reith gave one of his most revealing addresses to staff in Val Myer's new concert hall. To the men sitting in the centre, and to the women on either side, he said:

You came in response to an order issued, and you came as a staff. Would you try and listen to me as individuals, for I am going to try to talk to you for a very few moments as such; not as staff in the mass but as individuals? Now, in the front row there are the eighteen veteran survivors of the thirty-one who accompanied me into Savoy Hill on March 19th 1923. I felt I should like to have their moral support in the front row. … If there is anyone in this room who regrets leaving Savoy Hill, and who had a melancholy feeling on the last day there, I suppose it should be I, as I was the first to enter it, and actually it was I who found the place. But I have no regrets. I have affection for the old place; it was the scene of great labour and some achievement on the part of those who worked there; but I do not regret the past, because regretting the past is a great mistake. I look forward, and nothing but forward.

I suppose I have had three main functions since I joined the BBC: one is to resist attacks on the organization from without. They were considerable, and they are not altogether non-existent today. Another is to be on the lookout for ways and means of progress in our work. And the third is to ensure, if I can – and I mention it third accidentally, – it is of no less importance, to say the least of it, than the others – to ensure, if I can, the health and happiness of each one of you. With a big staff spread over several buildings I could not come in contact with a great many of you. It has been a perpetual distress to me, and some of you know me well enough to know that I don't say what I don't mean, to pass people in corridors and in the vicinity of our offices wondering whether or not they were members of our staff.

I will certainly know your names before I come in, and I shall know something about your work. Have you ever heard people say, or seen them write, that the BBC is a vast organization, and a pretty efficient one at that, but that there is rather too much of the machine – not quite enough soul? Well, we certainly are a big organization, but I am going to substitute for that word another and a better one. I prefer to look upon this Corporation as an organism rather than an organization; an organization may have little of the human element; not so an organism. We exist to provide programmes – that is why we were started and why we work, but no branch or department works to itself; no branch or department can do well without others, in fact the whole, benefiting; and no branch or department can do ill without affecting the whole. And an organism is a collection of individuals, and the health of one can affect, and, mind you, does affect, the health of the whole.

Reith wanted his staff to feel loyalty to the BBC, and during the next few weeks, he said, he proposed to visit everyone in his or her office. He had them carefully photographed, team by team, in the concert hall. The engineers were allowed to be pictured on the roof. There were between 650 and 700 people working in the building, including senior managers, middle managers, junior managers, secretaries,

Opposite, top The engineers were allowed to have their photograph taken outside, next to the aerials on the roof. The two highest masts carried the BBC's experimental ultra-short-wave transmissions. The third mast, at the front of the building, was spare and has never been used.

Opposite, bottom Broadcasting House was built at a time when London's architecture was changing dramatically. The smaller Georgian and Victorian buildings were being replaced by much larger steel-framed structures.

Broadcasting House was one of a large number of new buildings covered in Portland stone in a stripped classical style.

Below Reith (front row, fourth from right) and his staff, photographed in the concert hall. Reith later recalled that during the move from Magnet House to Savoy Hill his staff numbered just thirty-one, including 'a commissionaire, a cleaner and an office boy'. Nine years later, when he addressed them in the Broadcasting House concert hall, they had grown to 'about seven hundred'.

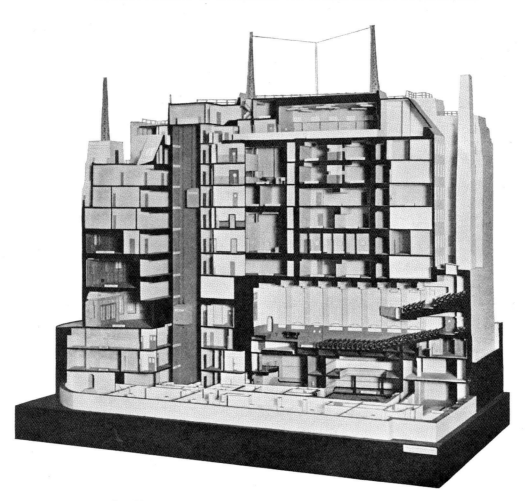

A cut-away model showing the differently sized rooms in the studio tower. The concert hall can be seen in the lower part of the model.

announcers, typists, bookkeepers, two in-house firemen, switchboard girls, post boys, finance department, legal department, publishing department, technical engineers, studio attendants, matron and catering staff.

Within the walls of Val Myer's building there was an extraordinary array of functions and uses, all stacked on top of one another. Broadcasting House was more like a small town; one visitor called it the 'Big House'. A cartoon (opposite, top left) from the *BBC Yearbook 1932* shows just how varied the activities in the building were on one floor alone. As well as the studios for different types of programme, there were the concert hall, the basement restaurant, the control room, general offices, executive offices, dressing-rooms, the post room, the battery room, listening-rooms, echo rooms, music control rooms, dramatic control rooms, the photographic room, the music library, the gramophone library, the library, rehearsal rooms and waiting-rooms. The rooms that had been squeezed into the building seemed endless. Behind the orderly-looking reception there was a warren of corridors, doors and staircases. The film *Death at Broadcasting House* (1934) accurately parodied the difficulties visitors had in negotiating the labyrinth of spaces. As one of the characters cried, 'It is a bit of a maze to let a pal loose in here.'

While Broadcasting House was being completed, licences were being bought at the rate of more than 1000 a day, and by 1934 the Post Office had issued 6.7 million, the equivalent of about 25 million listeners. There was huge demand – 50,000 applications alone in 1938 – to come into Broadcasting House to watch programmes being made, but the BBC allowed just one tour a day for a maximum of fifteen people

because of the problems of 'disturbance and congestion'. Most people had to wait nearly two years for a visit, although special consideration was given to overseas and provincial applications. The King and Queen, however, had no trouble getting in, and paid a visit on 7 July 1932.

For those who could get inside, the new building was a technical wonder, and boasted some impressive statistics. There were 800 doors, 6500 electric lamps, 98 clocks (all electrically synchronized from the new control room), 350 offices, 22 studios, 142 miles (230 km) of broadcasting circuit wiring and 660 thermionic valves. About half a mile (nearly 1 km) of Art Deco box light fittings provided artificial light to more than a mile (nearly 2 km) of corridors. Staff would be warmed by 840 radiators and could sit on the most modern chairs in the country. Around the building it was possible to see the designers' extraordinary attention to detail. McGrath had done an excellent job in co-ordinating the work. Telephones in the studios were recessed flush into the wall surfaces, with matching control-room and band-room buzzers mounted below, and the furniture and fittings were in harmony or standardized throughout. Even the gramophone players and forty loudspeakers in the building matched.

The last broadcast from Savoy Hill was made on 14 May 1932, a programme called *The End of Savoy Hill*. It ended with a voice announcing 'This is Broadcasting House calling', to mark the continuity of the service. To be in the new Broadcasting House during those first few months must have been truly exhilarating. One early visitor remarked: 'My lasting impression was that it was in a world of its own.

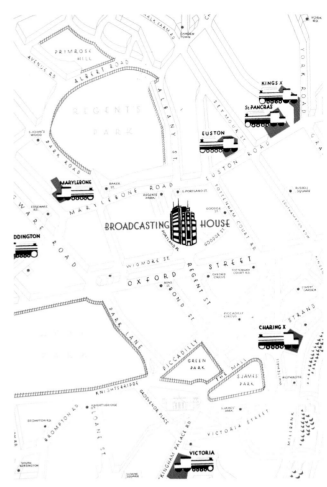

Above, left An early cartoon of a typical floor in Broadcasting House, showing the wide variety of departments and activities housed in the building.

Above, right A plan from the BBC's souvenir guidebook of 1932, showing Broadcasting House's central location and its proximity to the main London train stations.

Left Despite the huge range of functional requirements, all aspects of the interior were carefully considered. Furniture, clocks, lighting and technical equipment and signage were specially designed throughout.

Overleaf A wraparound sectional drawing from the souvenir guidebook of 1932, showing the many different uses that were shoe-horned into the building. The western side is to the left, and the eastern side to the right.

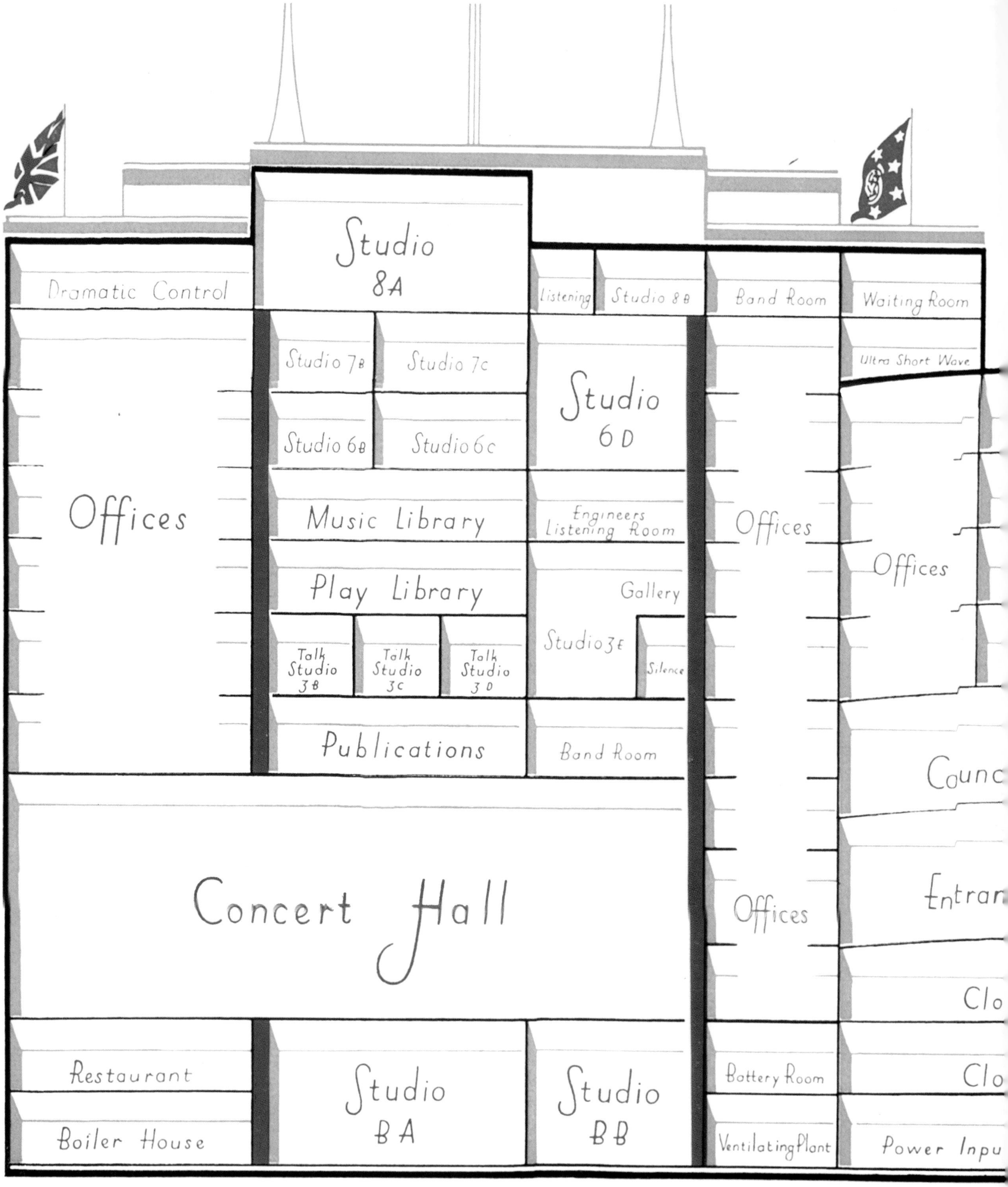

Studio
8A

Dramatic Control

Listening | Studio 8B | Band Room | Waiting Room

Studio 7B | Studio 7C

Ultra Short Wave

Studio
6D

Studio 6B | Studio 6C

Offices

Music Library

Engineers
Listening Room

Offices

Offices

Play Library

Gallery

Talk
Studio
3B | Talk
Studio
3C | Talk
Studio
3D | Studio 3E

Silence

Publications

Band Room

Counc

Concert Hall

Offices

Entran

Clo

Restaurant

Studio
BA

Studio
BB

Battery Room

Clo

Boiler House

Ventilating Plant

Power Inpu

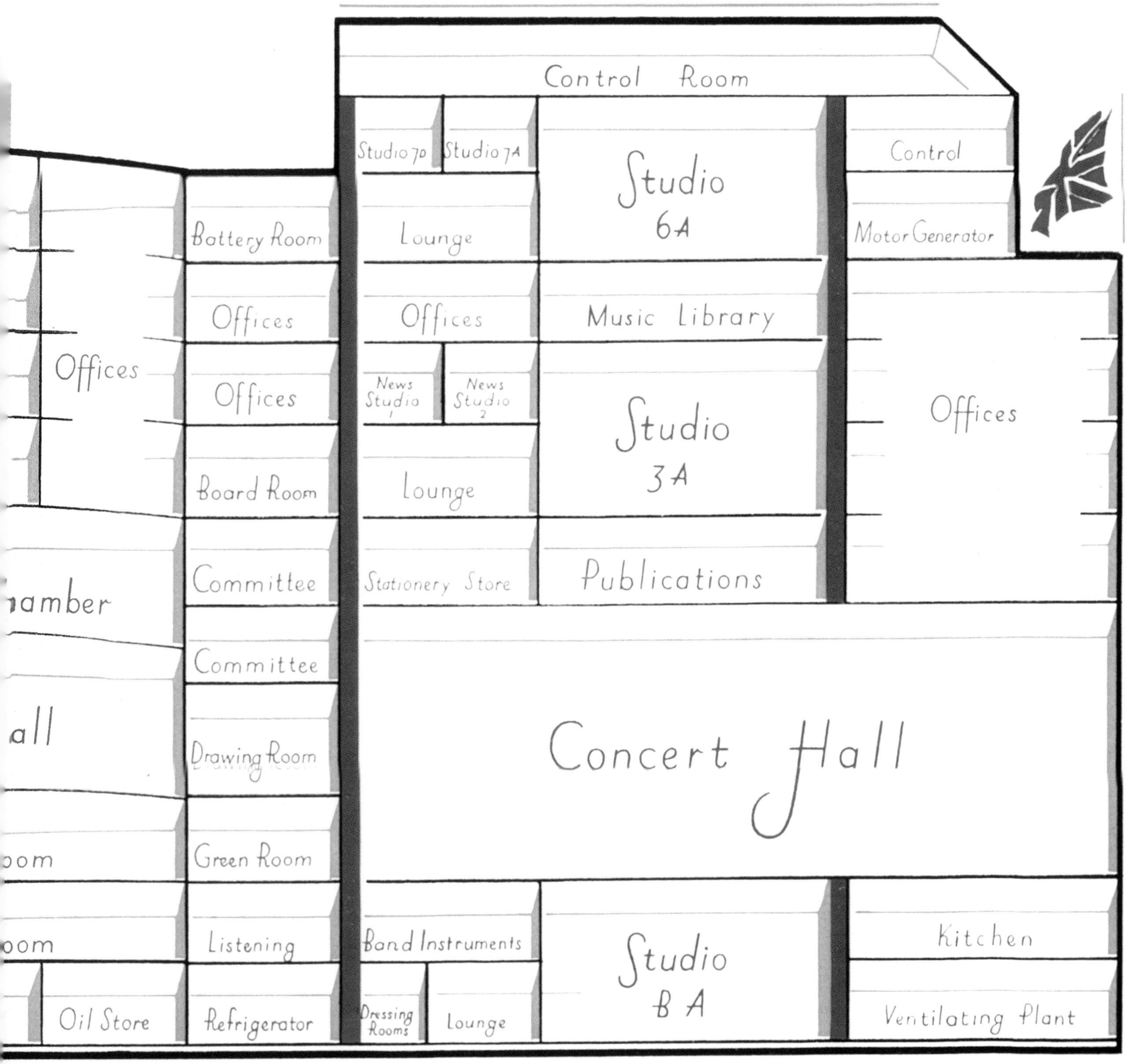

Control Room

Studio 7o | Studio 7A

Control

Studio
6A

Motor Generator

Battery Room

Lounge

Offices

Offices

Music Library

Offices

Offices

News Studio 1 | News Studio 2

Studio
3A

Board Room

Lounge

Offices

Committee

Stationery Store

Publications

Committee

Concert Hall

Drawing Room

Chamber

Green Room

Hall

Listening

Band Instruments

Kitchen

oom

Studio
8A

oom

Oil Store

Refrigerator

Dressing Rooms | Lounge

Ventilating Plant

47

Below Flowers played an important part in the decor of Broadcasting House. They helped to relax nervous guests and provided a splash of colour in the otherwise sparsely decorated spaces.

Below, right The entrance hall was designed by Val Myer and lined with Hopton-Wood stone, or 'English marble', from Derbyshire. Reminiscent of a banking hall, it helped to give the impression of an established, efficient and orderly organization. The small reception desk was sandwiched between stone-clad columns that define Val Myer's original ideal semi-circular space.

Opposite The building was soon a hive of activity. The first few years of its life were captured by Mark Oliver Dell and H.L. Wainwright, official photographers to the *Architectural Review* from 1930 to 1946. Their striking and uncompromising imagery did much to promote the Modern architectural movement in Britain. Using dramatic viewpoints and imaginative lighting techniques, they included BBC staff of all ranks, including workers in the busy post room and the army of cleaners.

I felt when I was inside it that it was the nerve centre of the larger world outside with vibrations reaching out to the farthest island.' George Posford, who had worked as an arranger and accompanist at Savoy Hill, wrote a piece of music that, according to Colin Reid's *Action Stations: A History of Broadcasting House* (1987), 'caught the spirit and atmosphere of the whole place'. Mark Oliver Dell and H.L. Wainwright's photographs managed to capture admirably the sparse spatial character of the interior and the diversity of its new population.

An early glimpse of life in Broadcasting House can be seen in a Post Office-made film called *BBC: The Voice of Britain*, which was shot in June 1934. At 6 am an army of cleaners would arrive and register at reception. They would have their names ticked off on a long list and would take two-and-a-half hours to scrub about 1750 steps, fill every inkwell and clean the building from top to bottom. At 8.30 a number of clerks would arrive to sort the first postal delivery for the various departments. More than 2000 letters would pour into the post room every day. Young page boys buzzed through the building in smart blue serge suits, black ties and stiff white collars, delivering to in-trays and collecting from out-trays every forty-five minutes. By 1937 there was no shortage of willing volunteers wanting to work for the BBC: the waiting-list for charwomen, for example, was said to be around 3000. There were ninety-five boys, who joined the BBC at fourteen years old and had to attend evening school as a condition of employment. The BBC paid two-thirds of their school fees and gave them a dress allowance of half a crown (the equivalent of about £4.50) a week.

For Reith, presentation was still important, and the BBC flag was hoisted every day at 9.30 am and struck at 6 pm. Inside, Lady Allen (Eric Gill's sister) supervised the important regular delivery of flowers. These were placed carefully to bring colour into the plain interior and to help to put nervous guests at ease. In his book *By-ways of the BBC* (1938), Wilfrid Goatman claimed that 'the massed blooms and ingeniously arranged branches impress many visitors even more than the mysteries of the control room'. Flowers were fresh every day in the studios and waiting-rooms, too, and were also placed on the roof terraces, providing Regent Street with a splash of seasonal colour: daffodils in the spring, geraniums in the summer and chrysanthemums in the autumn and winter.

Lord Gerald Wellesley, a Fellow of the Royal Institute of British Architects, went further in suggesting that flowers were an important part of the interior decoration:

The thrill that a vase of flowers or a cactus gives in the setting of a modern room is unexpected and difficult to analyse. It is like a living, articulate voice in a well of silence. It is the one note which breaks the repose, the one place where rowdy colour flashes and exuberant forms are allowed. Place the same vase on a table in some old-fashioned drawing room and it would not be noticed. The use of flowers and plants in Broadcasting House is masterly and in many cases forms an essential element in the decorative scheme.

The performers would enter through their own entrance, the 'artists' lobby', where the information boards would describe exactly what was going on that day in each studio. It was

49

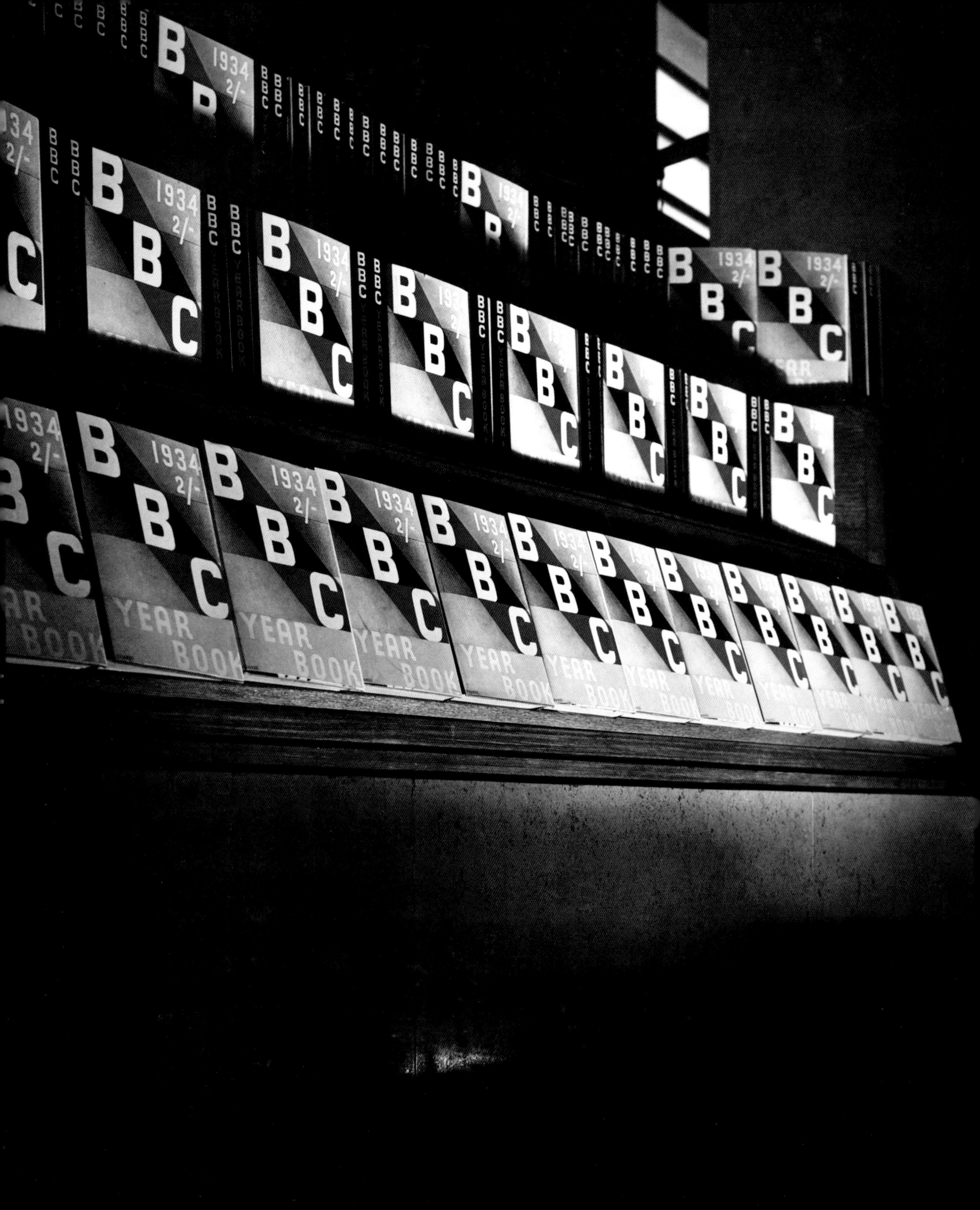
B
1934
2/-
B
C
YEAR
BOOK
BBC YEAR BOOK

important that artists should be made to feel as relaxed as possible, and they would be escorted by the smartly dressed page boys smoothly and comfortably to the waiting-rooms by the studios, 'in order that the best result may be obtained'. 'Every performer is governed by matters of temperament, but in the carefully regulated atmosphere, discreet decoration, and simplified equipment, of the modern studios at Broadcasting House, there is no reason why any artist after slight adjustment to [their] surroundings, should not feel completely at ease.'

The design of the reception, lifts, staircases, corridors and offices gave the appearance of efficient and functional organization. There were no fewer than six lifts in the building, and they were some of the fastest in the capital, with the capacity to carry up to twenty-four people at 400 feet (120 m) per minute. Everything, including the books on the shelves,

was neatly arranged. Val Myer's stripped classical designs for the reception, council chamber and concert hall provided an interesting contrast with the almost shockingly sparse approach of the younger designers and their modern functionalism.

The studios

Through sound proof doors, and doors, and doors again you come to an inside core of the building, isolated from all the rest, where the makers of the noises practise to make them good noises.
Film, BBC: *The Voice of Britain*, 1934

Whatever reservations there may have been about the overall success of the outside of the building, the twenty-two studios hidden away inside Val Myer's tower were undoubtedly very

Opposite Even the most mundane of subjects, such as a row of books, with its geometric and almost architectural quality, was deemed worthy of the attention of photographers Dell and Wainwright.

Above The *Architectural Review* of August 1932 was devoted to Broadcasting House, and featured colour photographs for the first time in the magazine's history. The images convey the qualities of McGrath's extraordinary miniature theatre (the vaudeville studio) in the basement.

special. The designers had managed to transform the dozens of oddly shaped rooms within the tower, and had conjured up a series of magically atmospheric spaces. Part of their quirkiness and appeal was that no room in the studio tower was a plain rectangle. Traditionally decorated spaces were definitely not an option.

The simply furnished and brightly coloured rooms contained cutting-edge furniture, and perhaps just two or three simple objects: a vase filled with flowers, one picture or a statuette on a table. 'Bright' bands were given bright rooms, while 'talkers' were provided with intimate little studios. Broadcasting House combined form and function in perfect harmony: the different uses of the studios inspired the decoration, which was designed to stimulate the performers. The designers also brought their own personalities to their work: McGrath's was playful, while Chermayeff's was robust: he was said to 'use materials boldly and [have] an interesting sense of colour'. Wells Coates had been made responsible for rooms of a more technical nature, such as the control room and the news studios. Staff spent longer in these spaces, and accordingly they were more 'neutral' and architecturally 'serious'. Compared to Savoy Hill, noise breakout between adjoining studios had been minimized, and there was already a noticeable improvement in sound production. The Savoy Hill studios had been made acoustically dead, with practically no reverberation, but Broadcasting House was much more 'lively', and allowed a brighter and more natural acoustic effect.

As we have seen, traditional suppliers had been coaxed into producing new products and materials, and two years after the building opened McGrath reflected on the wider importance of the new studios in Broadcasting House, describing what had been done as 'architecting rather than decorating'. 'The necessarily clean result', he said, 'has set an excellent example for interior work other than studios.' Speaking nearly fifty years later, in 1972, he reinforced the wider importance of Broadcasting House to industrial design: 'The designs for the BBC gave the first real fillip to industrial design in England[,] and Wells Coates, Serge Chermayeff and myself were three of the first architects to work in that field in London.'

Wellesley described their achievement: 'The interior of Broadcasting House is the most important example of untraditional decoration yet completed in this country. The accumulated rubbish or wisdom of the ages has been washed away, and something which is definitely and entirely new has taken its place. Such a phenomenon has never occurred before in the world's history.'

The 'voice of the world'

Nowadays, there are more facts to know and more influences to appreciate. The microphone has provided a new means for distributing opinion and knowledge to millions of listeners.
Film, BBC: The Voice of Britain, 1934

The mixed architectural styles of Broadcasting House suggested a period of transition from an established old order to a new, more complex, modern era. The BBC had moved from an almost cosy world of improvisation and 'making do' at Savoy Hill to a large 'factory' and the business of sound

production. In doing so it had become a patron of architecture and set new standards for quality. The *Architectural Review* concluded that an example comparable to that of the London Underground (in Charles Holden's 55 Broadway building of 1929) had been set, and congratulated Reith on using 'the best modern architects in the country'. Assistant Controller Goldsmith, chairman of the Studio Decoration Committee, especially, had 'shown foresight and courage worthy of the best traditions of the BBC'.

The building was not perfect, but the organization could be said to have set an example to all public institutions in the country, as J.M. Richards noted in 1940: 'The BBC can take credit for bringing modern architecture into the inside of its building, whatever the outside; for in the early days of modern architecture, [the Corporation] gave the first encouragement [the movement] received from any official body by employing a team of the best young designers for the interior equipment and furnishing of studios and offices.'

The first big event in the new building's history was the start of the Empire Service, a first venture into overseas broadcasting. This was launched on 19 December 1932 and inaugurated on Christmas Day with an hour of greetings from all parts of the empire, followed by King George V's Christmas Day message, which praised the service as 'one of the marvels of modern science'. He went on: 'I am enabled this Christmas day to speak to all my peoples throughout the empire. I take it as a good omen that wireless should have reached its present perfection at a time when the empire has been linked in close union. For it offers us immense possibilities to make that union closer still.'

In less than ten years the BBC had gone from thirty-one employees at Savoy Hill to its own state-of-the-art headquarters with around 700 staff broadcasting to the empire. The 'voice of Britain' had become the 'voice of the world'.

A Tour of Broadcasting House in the Early 1930s

As far as the newspapers are concerned ... the BBC has become news.
Tom Clarke, *Daily Mail*, 17 January 1932

The completion of Broadcasting House marked a turning point for the BBC. By the time the building had opened, the idea of radio had become firmly lodged in the public consciousness. Reith's struggle to establish the BBC was over, and Broadcasting House would allow the organization to enter, as the historian Asa Briggs put it, 'a period of enrichment and extension'.

Immediately after its completion Broadcasting House was repeatedly visited, written about, filmed and photographed. It was without precedent: simultaneously office, studio, theatre, laboratory, restaurant, library and temple. In the numerous rooms there could be seen an extraordinary array of spaces, colours and materials. Colourful, modern studios sat alongside panelled rooms that reflected a desire for institutional gravitas; the old world and the new could be seen side by side.

The move would signal a change in the programmes being made. Many working in the new building wanted to develop and transform the public's taste or, as some thought, even revolutionize opinion. But, as Briggs also pointed out, the output of Broadcasting House between the wars would console as well as inspire. A few days after Broadcasting House opened, on 11 May 1932, *Punch* magazine summed it up: 'Consoling voices of the air/ Soothing the sightless, cheering the bedridden./ The lighthouse watchers, men who bravely bear/ The burden of captivity unbidden –/ Voices that calm the heart and ease the strain/ Of those who live in loneliness or pain.'

This chapter takes us through some of the original interiors of Broadcasting House. We start as the BBC souvenir book of 1932 did, at the top of the building, and work our way down. The images offer a fascinating insight into the taste of the period, and in them we can see the variety of people and spaces needed to allow the BBC to operate, from calm engineers in the laboratory-like control room in the roof, to flamboyant drama producers and dance bands in the brightly coloured basement studios.

Eighth floor

The control room The large, open space at the top of the building was designed by Wells Coates. It was a well-lit room within the roof, and divided functionally into two areas: one for transmissions, the other for rehearsals. The idea was that a single person would be able to control the operation remotely and oversee the technical quality of programmes. Eight desks were provided for programme rehearsals, and the transmission section was equipped with six desks. The transmissions area contained much subsidiary equipment, such as amplifiers, control apparatus, switch gear, wireless check receivers, landline testing equipment and the Greenwich Time Signal apparatus. The fact that the room had adequate stand-by equipment was a great improvement on Savoy Hill. The power supply was by means of batteries that were duplicated throughout for resilience, providing a back-up supply, and the room was connected by a landline to Brookmans Park Transmitting Station, from where the broadcasts were put on air.

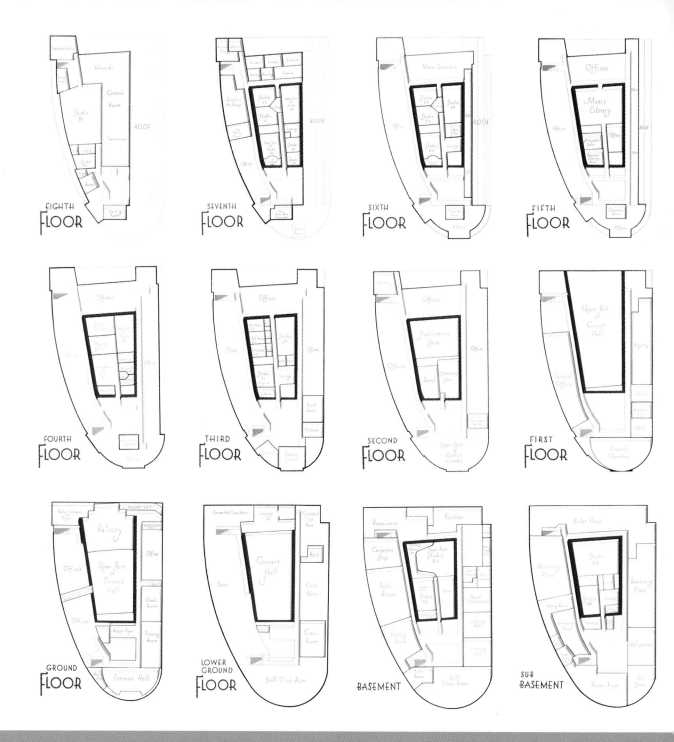

EIGHTH **FLOOR**

SEVENTH **FLOOR**

SIXTH **FLOOR**

FIFTH **FLOOR**

FOURTH **FLOOR**

THIRD **FLOOR**

SECOND **FLOOR**

FIRST **FLOOR**

GROUND **FLOOR**

LOWER GROUND **FLOOR**

BASEMENT

SUB BASEMENT

'Well, have these plans given you any idea of the geography of Broadcasting House?'
'No, Sir.'
'Good, I thought not!'
Film, *Death at Broadcasting House*, 1934

The new building was a maze, and the film *Death at Broadcasting House* made a number of direct references to its confusing layout. The confusion arose partly because of the internal staircase and lifts that served the studios separately. It was hard to work out where one was on any floor, or even the direction in which one was going.

The series of plans above shows the basic layout of Broadcasting House in 1932. The (not quite semicircular) curved prow facing Regent Street is at the bottom of each plan. Immediately obvious is the studio tower at the centre of each floor. The diagrams show how the huge numbers of rooms have been squeezed into the tightly packed spaces and how the usable space in the roof gradually disappears on the Langham Street (right-hand) side of the building.

Studio 8A: Military band studio

The first studio to be completed in Broadcasting House was Serge Chermayeff's military band studio, 8A. It was the only studio in the building to have natural light, and had a streamlined shape with curved corners and horizontal strips of buff Donnacona building board separated by white metal joints. The colours were subdued, and the cork floor laid in five subtle shades, from light buff to black. The only notes of vibrant colour were the settees, which were covered in striped coral-red fabric, and the doors, which were faced with oak ply and sprayed with brilliant blue–green cellulose paint. A large circle in the centre of the studio marked the location for the band. Banjo-shaped objects on the ceiling combined ventilation and lighting, and side light boxes avoided shadows in the room; the pattern of the light fittings picked up on the painted cork floor. The skirting boards were removable, to provide access for microphone wiring, and the polished aluminium-alloy door handles and other metalwork in the studio were specially designed to be resistant to perspiration. Mounted high on the wall was a stainless-steel clock, 3 feet (1 m) in diameter, with anodized copper hour markings and matt-black hands, and minute markings engraved and filled with wax. The tubular chromium-plated steel-frame settees and conductor's rostrum were also designed by Chermayeff; the rostrum was adjustable, with a revolving seat.

Because of its large size, the studio was used almost immediately for all types of music and vaudeville performance. The *BBC Yearbook 1933* stated that 'the opening broadcast by Henry Hall's BBC Dance Band took place in not very favourable circumstances', because studio 8A 'had been designed, and is now used for, quite different musical combinations'. Hall's appointment in the first week of 1932 was greeted with some reservations because of his apparent lack of showmanship, especially as he was following in the footsteps of the popular band leader Jack Payne. Some critics thought Hall was hampered by his Salvation Army background. The original broadcast alone brought in around 1000 letters containing suggestions and criticism.

Studio 8B The small debates
studio was an informal, cosy, intimate
space designed to encourage
relaxed conversation among a
small number of people. It is almost
domestic in character, with soft
chairs, flowers, a lampshade and
a fireplace. Stan Laurel and Oliver
Hardy are pictured looking relaxed
at the Serge Chermayeff-designed
horseshoe-shaped debates table.
The design allowed the microphone
to stand comfortably in the centre
of the table.

Dramatic control rooms There
were two dramatic control rooms
on the eighth floor, both designed by
Wells Coates. The rooms could be
used for rehearsals or transmissions.
Each had a dramatic control desk,
a loudspeaker, a telephone (for
communication with the control
room) and a microphone. The
producer could give instructions
during rehearsals to all the artists
in the studios via the microphone
and loudspeakers, and, during
transmissions, to the production
staff responsible for the studios
by means of headphones. Facilities
were also provided to enable artists
not immediately required in the

production to listen to the play. The use of many studios for one production meant that staff were dispersed over various floors, making it necessary to have 'studio managers' (in the theatre sense of stage managers) to keep track of artists and make sure not only that they reacted to the right cue light but also that they were in the correct studio.

Indicators for 'return cue lights' were used in studios to allow the drama producers to cue performers when required. Lights were also placed over the entrances and exits to the studios. There were four colours, plus white. Outside the studios, a yellow light indicated that a studio was in use, while a red light showed that a studio was being used for a final broadcast. Inside the studios, lobbies and listening-rooms, a blue light meant that a microphone was being used for a rehearsal. Green lights were used in larger studios to cue artists, while a white light indicated 'You are wanted on the telephone'.

Dramatic control panels Using music and different sound effects, the ambition of the drama producer was to create pictures in the mind. This led to the early observation that 'as a medium, wireless is superior to television because the pictures are better'. But in order to do this, the drama team had to be able to make convincing sound effects. In addition to manual effects, technical innovations and sophisticated electronic effects opened up new possibilities. As drama productions grew more complex, producers demanded both more control over the sound quality and more studios within the building.

The dramatic control panels (DCPs) allowed more complex dramas than would have been possible if the sound effects and performers had had to be accommodated and stage-managed from one studio. Scenes that needed different acoustics needed different studios. The new panels meant that the shouts of a crowd, gunfire, speech and a background of military music could be broadcast simultaneously without all the performers being in one space, and enabled drama producers to control the output of half the studios in the building at once. The mixed programme could then be passed to the control room

for distribution to the various transmitters. DCP nos. 1 and 2 had a rather space-age appearance: they were battleship grey, with knobs and switches, and flashing red lights that glowed as studios faded in and out. It was also claimed that DCP no. 3 had a sliding seat to make it easier to move quickly along it.

Death at Broadcasting House was a novel that was turned into a film and released in November 1934. Eric Maschwitz, Director of Variety, and Val Gielgud, head of the BBC's newly formed drama department (and John Gielgud's brother), borrowed the plans of Broadcasting House to ensure accuracy, and wrote the play

while on holiday together in the south of France. It was a rather hammy whodunnit, in which a murderer strangles an actor on the radio. In the film, Val Gielgud (second from right) is shown managing a mix on the revolutionary 'dramatic control panel' inside Broadcasting House. Although Gielgud had the very latest technical equipment, the film itself was less successful, as a contemporary critic remarked: 'The overdone mystique of sound broadcasting is amply demonstrated by the studio histrionics of the genuine Head of Drama, Val Gielgud, who can only blame himself: he also wrote the story.'

By 1934 there was a feeling that these new technologies had been slightly over-publicized, and the problem was to find the content, or, to put it another way, decent plays. It seemed nothing could beat a straightforward broadcast of 'songs from the shows' or Jack Payne's popular dance band.

Seventh floor

The music control room This space contained a music control panel, which allowed musically qualified staff to listen to the music on an adjacent loudspeaker and, with a score in hand, monitor the quality of the performance. One of the specially designed matching loudspeaker cabinets can be seen on the right.

The telephone exchange
Fitted with 650 extensions, the exchange handled an extraordinary 11,000 internal calls a day. Staff throughout the building frequently moved offices, and the switchboard staff had to be familiar with where people were sitting. The exchange was connected by private lines to other BBC offices in London and to the homes of senior management. Around 1900 external calls a day were made or received.

The six original switchboard positions were soon doubled to twelve. The twenty-six staff also handled enquiries from members of the public – some to settle bets or confirm the pronunciation of disputed words.

In 1923 BBC staff had made 25,000 local calls (i.e. within the London telephone area) and received about 20,000. After only five years in Broadcasting House, staff were making 474,450 calls annually, and receiving 375,000.

Blattnerphones Broadcasting House's state-of-the-art equipment included the Blattnerphones (early tape recorders), stored on the seventh floor. The machine pictured above is a later model, installed at Maida Vale in January 1934.

The Blattnerphone was invaluable. 'It helped teach a broadcaster more about his own faults by letting him listen to himself for quarter of an hour than is possible by direct criticism of any length.' It enabled actors to have a rehearsal played back to them, and allowed a conductor to hear the previous night's performance.

To early broadcasters the technology must have seemed

magical. One employee gasped: 'No one recognizes his own voice when he first hears it from the loud speaker.' A spool of steel tape was 1 mile (1.6 km) long and weighed 21 lb (10 kg), but only gave a recording time of around twenty minutes. A second machine allowed the switching together of two recordings, and by the end of 1932 a half-hour programme could be recorded. By 1934 twenty tapes a week were being recorded and transmitted, at first for re-broadcasting national and regional programmes in different time zones for the Empire Service, keeping the Blattnerphones busy for up to seventeen hours a day.

Unfortunately, the machines were noisy and had irregular tape speed, so considerable effort was needed to keep them working, and this had an impact on the number of bookings that could be fulfilled. They were gradually taken out of service during 1935 and replaced by more advanced machines, such as the Marconi Stille system. Both machines allowed playback soon after recording, as (unlike disc recording) neither system required any post-recording processing.

Sixth floor

The ten studios on the sixth and seventh floors in the Productions group of studios were designed by Wells Coates and mainly used for drama. The largest was 6A; 6B, 6C, 7A, 7B and 7C were smaller and used for speech. Rooms 6D (opposite) and 7D were effects studios, with water tanks and other effects equipment, and 6E and 7E were used solely for gramophone effects and incidental music. Studios 6C, 6D, 7A, 7C and 7D had a totally dead acoustic and were generally linked to the dramatic control panels.

Studio 6D: Dramatic effects studio One of the most impressive spaces in the building, this studio was said to be 'as exciting as a magician's cave'. In the centre of the room was a specially designed table that was divided into six sections, each with a different surface finish on which various sounds could be reproduced by friction. The table could be rotated, raised or lowered to bring it closer to other sound-effects equipment. The early sound-effects methods were inventive, to say the least.

Wind rushing through trees in a forest was best represented by shovelling coal on a steel floor, and a fountain playing was simulated by

the sound of the continuous smashing of glass. Running a rollerskate along a riveted tin bath was used to make train noises, and a pound of potatoes and a big drum were used to create a realistic-sounding avalanche. There were wind machines, suspended metal sheets and drums for simulating thunder, and a compressed-air machine for wind effects. Two small boxes made electrical noises, and a large water tank could reproduce the sound of a small stream or the roar of a waterfall. One area was dedicated to making railway noises and another to the rattling and slamming of doors. Even the floor of the studio had different finishes

of carpet, wood and concrete for creating different acoustic effects. The microphones suspended from the ceiling and operated with two long, jointed arms could be placed beside any effect. Because of all the equipment in the room, the lower part of the studio walls was protected with a grey rubber dado, perforated with 1-inch-diameter (2.5 cm) holes to help it retain its acoustic properties.

The *BBC Yearbook 1933* hinted at the fun yet to be had in the dramatic effects studio: 'The acoustic differences between Savoy Hill and BH were about 100 per cent, and the potentialities [of this space] are not likely to be explored for some time

to come. There is no doubt that the knowledge of the perspective of sound in the production of plays has by no means reached its limits.'

Fifth floor

The music library The music library had at Magnet House been stored on the kitchen range. It was now situated on the fifth floor of Broadcasting House, and held scores for more than 10,500 orchestral works, military band parts for 4000 pieces of music and 32,000 vocal scores. It was said to be the largest library of its kind in the world, and contained almost anything from comic songs to handwritten parts of Bach cantatas. In September 1933 a recorded programmes section opened. This contained around 25,000 records divided into four sections: commercial records, dance music, foreign records and 'waxes' (wax recordings from the Blattnerphones). Two copies of every record were held, one for rehearsal and one for transmission, although both were needed when broadcasting a tune that took up both sides of a disc without a break. Dance records were generally thrown away, unless they had 'caught the popular mood' or in some way 'expressed the spirit of the moment', in which case they were kept in the 'museum' library.

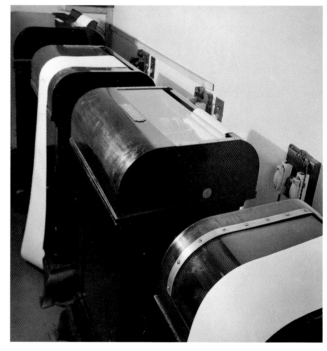

Fourth floor

News studios 4A and 4B The *BBC Handbook 1931* promised that the building's twenty-two studios would include 'a small apartment necessary for news', and sang the praises of 'an interesting unit' on the fourth floor, 'designed specifically for the reading of news bulletins and emergency broadcasts of gramophone records', in case transmission was interrupted. Wells Coates designed the two news studios, which, at 12 × 7 feet (3.7 × 2 m), were the smallest in Broadcasting House and were separated by a lobby. The news

editor sat in this small space and was able to prepare late news items and pass them through to the announcer while the bulletin was being read. The desks and furniture in the two studios were curved so that the announcer could swivel on a chair between reading notes and playing records.

Once seated in the news studio, the announcers would check unusual pronunciations and decide who would read which bulletin. They would speak into the Wells Coates-designed microphone with its 'lazy-tong' suspension, which meant that it could be brought closer to the presenter's lips. The curved walls were specially finished by a furniture

upholsterer in a silver–grey hemp and artificial silk fabric. The walls and ceiling were painted a complementary dove-grey colour, and the furniture was made from laminated board veneered with Australian walnut. The public regarded the early newsreaders with some affection, so much so, an early chronicler of the BBC reported, that 'an announcer could not cough during a broadcast without receiving presents of everything from cough-lozenges to woollen underwear'.

The news-agency tape machines in the adjacent newsroom were busy churning out tape day and night. A specially made large waste bin was

installed near the machines, and was said to be 'one of the most valuable assistants in this task of preparing the bulletins'.

A NATIONAL S.O.S.

"Help us to help ourselves"

The Transformation.

360 BEDS IN THE HOSPITAL FOR Crippled Children from all parts of the country.

50 PLACES IN THE COLLEGE WHERE Crippled Lads from 14 to 16 years of age are trained in skilled handicrafts.

The greatest assistance humanity can give to crippled children is to fit them for useful life with every chance of becoming physically normal citizens. **410** crippled children are undergoing treatment and training at the Lord Mayor Treloar Cripples Hospital and College. Funds urgently needed to maintain this national work.

If you are a lover of children, or are blessed with bonny youngsters of your own, please send a contribution to assist in restoring those less fortunate to health and happiness.

LORD MAYOR TRELOAR CRIPPLES HOSPITAL & COLLEGE,

ALTON and HAYLING ISLAND BRANCH.

To THE SECRETARY,
    25 ELY PLACE, LONDON, E.C.1.

I enclose a Cheque/Postal Order for £.................
as a contribution to the Lord Mayor Treloar Cripples Hospital and College.

Signature ....

Address ....

B.B.C. ....

SOS and good causes The BBC's SOS service, also broadcast from the news studios, was for contacting people in emergencies if all other forms of communication had failed. Many thought it part of the BBC's public service remit; others saw it as a waste of time, although, rather astonishingly, more than 50 per cent of the broadcasts were actually successful. One message in 1933 gave warning that a shopkeeper had supplied a customer with petrol instead of paraffin, and another that a boy had been sold live cartridges rather than blanks (not by the same shopkeeper, one hopes). Both petrol and cartridges were safely recovered.

Broadcast descriptions of missing persons (usually children or the 'mentally deranged') were not quite so successful, and were stopped altogether in the same year. There were also Sunday broadcasts on behalf of charities. Wireless clubs (called radio circles) raised money for children's causes, and appeals were broadcast from the children themselves, with follow-up advertisements placed in the BBC yearbooks.

The office of the Director of Programmes Even the more traditional-looking panelled rooms in Broadcasting House had no unnecessary decoration. McGrath designed the room of the Director of Programmes, Roger Eckersley, in English walnut, and covered his chairs in Nigerian goatskin. Eckersley's desk had concealed lighting and a secret swivelling device that cleverly hid the telephone.

Third floor

The Director-General's office

Reith and most of his fellow managers were located at the southern, curved end of the building, with views down Regent Street. Their status was marked by curtains in their rooms and carpet (not linoleum) on the floor. The walls were simply panelled, without elaborate decoration, or, as Reilly commented in the *BBC Yearbook 1933*, 'free from the loops of carved fruit and flowers our bankers still require for complete happiness'. Reith's own office had a flower-decked balcony instead. The focal point in his simple oak-panelled room was a fireplace surround from Wyatt's Foley House. A richly upholstered suite of furniture in pink satin and a rug designed in the shape of a compass rose were later installed by Reith. The latter apparently 'needed to be put back accurately' after being cleaned or beaten.

The 'talks' studio waiting-room
Separated from the corridor by a wool curtain that was coloured buff and grey, with stripes of vermilion and blue, the waiting-room contained a curved settee that was said to be 'particularly comfortable'. The settee and chairs were upholstered in a coral tweed fabric, and the carpet was by Marion Dorn (1896–1964). It was protected by a bell-shaped ashtray, which was 'impossible' to overturn. By July 1934 the carefully designed furniture had been removed and replaced with leather chairs.

Studio 3A: *Children's Hour*
An early version of *Children's Hour* had started in late 1922, using imaginary aunts and uncles as presenters. The programme was in fact forty-four minutes long, and was broadcast between 5.15 and 5.59 pm, when the children were bid goodnight. According to the *BBC Yearbook 1933*, its ingredients were 'quiet and recreative amusement, the presentation of beauty in music, drama and poetry, the discreet and agreeable introduction of a little information and an occasional precept'. The double-height studio, with its Donnacona-boarded walls, was overlooked by the listening-room above. The constant drive to improve the performance in the studios can be seen in the decision to leave the third-floor children's studio, and the 'talks' studios on the sixth and seventh floors, partly unfinished, to allow for further research and development.

Announcing-rooms Studios were provided with an adjacent announcing-room, or silence room. This allowed the announcer to take control of a programme and make announcements during intervals, without disturbing the artists in the studio itself. A telephone connected the announcer to the control room, and signal lights were installed to convey instructions to performers in the studios.

Studios 3B, 3C, 3D: 'Talks' In the early years of Broadcasting House, an amazing array of unrehearsed debates was broadcast by the Talks department from the third floor, and from the basement vaudeville studio, where they took place in front of a small audience. An early series of programmes featured pairs of firemen, policemen and bricklayers from different countries in conversation. The department also broadcast short talks and lectures, normally given by just one or two people. One such – Joe Patts, parish clerk of Ilford for sixty-one years – is pictured above, in 1935. The studios were designed by Chermayeff and were

interesting examples of functionalism applied to a more intimate use.

Each studio had its own decorative scheme, of simple, muted colours. Wellesley said of the rooms in his article in the *BBC Yearbook 1933* that 'the lights are shaded, the furniture is comfortable with a comfort which one feels is produced by a profound study of anatomy . . . . The rooms seem to induce bodily well being and mental alertness. Here one feels is a setting in which lean-faced scientists can discuss relativity, or the more intellectual members of the communist party the ideal distribution of wealth.'

Even the least self-conscious person often found it hard to relax

when chatting to several million listeners. A BBC yearbook article of 1934 by John Gloag entitled 'Learning to Broadcast' gives some insight into the art:

You go too fast at first: Then you go too slow. Then you emphasize the wrong words, until you suddenly realize why you are so disgustingly self conscious and unnatural. You are trying to be conversational to an audience you can't see with material that is wholly unconversational in form. You are reading something that was written either to be printed and read, or to be spoken from a platform. First of all, you learn to avoid long and complicated

words. You cut out every needless word above two syllables. You study the ends of each sentence, and take care that you don't finish with words of awkward or ambiguous sound. You take particular care that in your typed manuscript 'do not' is rendered as 'don't', and 'cannot' as 'can't'. Otherwise in reading you may unconsciously become unbearably stilted.

Speak slowly, for you will never before the microphone speak quite as slowly as you think you are speaking. Feel about for your words, not theatrically, but with the natural pauses that everyone makes in conversation . . .

Visualize a few of the people whom you know will be listening; picture

them in their armchairs, and try to be conversational with them . . . . Let your voice play about as it normally would, and make gestures with your hands. That helps create the illusion of the audience.

Before broadcasting was invented nobody had ever had such opportunities for boring simultaneously so large a number of people, or helping them to appreciate and enjoy something that you think should be appreciated and enjoyed.

Studio 3E: Religious studio

The daily service was broadcast at 10.15 am. The very first service started with a simple blessing:

Here is a quiet room,
Pause for a little space
And without faithless gloom
With joy upon thy face
Pray for God's grace.

The religious studio was designed by Edward Maufe, who had been instructed to create a temple where 'Catholic and Calvinist, Jew and Moslem should feel equally at home', or, as a contemporary observer put it, a 'Temple to an Unknown God'.

It was a large, double-height space, overlooked by a balcony, and contained a desk, a grand piano and a clock. A table and six chairs were provided for a choir. The east end of the studio was supported on four slender, hollow, green columns with silver and gold capitals. In the centre of a tall arch was a brilliantly illuminated cyclorama, with a backcloth of the 'palest blue' to convey an impression of infinite distance across the silver altar. The floors and Tentest-board walls were pink. The colour was said to be 'very happy'. The walls were finished with a special acoustic plaster and the ceiling delicately embossed with stars and crescent moons, coloured blue with spangles of gold. A backlit recess above the balcony ceiling created the illusion of sky. A vase of flowers stood in a white alcove, and during services a cross was projected on to the white background above. A statue of St George by Vernon Hill (1887–1972) stood in a niche next to the piano.

Listeners soon made it clear, however, that they preferred to feel 'the atmosphere of an actual church', and to know they were part of a real congregation. By 1933 very few of the BBC's religious broadcasts were made from the religious studio.

Studio 3D: Library 'talks' studio

'As a concession to the conservatism and weakness of human nature,' as Wellesley put it in the *BBC Yearbook 1933*, it was decided by the Studio Decoration Committee that one of the 'talks' studios should be traditional in style. It was feared that 'elderly dons and clergymen, so far from being stimulated and put at their best by the naked simplicity of functionalism and metal furniture, would be frightened of it.' To put the elderly 'talkers' at ease the committee requested a design that would be reminiscent of a 'small and quiet library, which might be found in an old town or country house'.

Goldsmith, in charge of the Decoration Committee, proudly stated that this was the only historic form of decoration in the studios. The room was designed by Dorothy Warren Trotter and had a picture of George Washington over the fireplace, suggesting that it was used occasionally for talks to America. A false window was dressed with curtains, to hint at a view outside, and the chair had been 'previously used by [novelist] Arnold Bennett'.

Second floor

The library A small library was provided on the Portland Place side of the building. It could be found at the end of the corridor and was furnished with apple-green steel shelving.

First floor

The general office Describing the building in the *BBC Yearbook 1933*, Reilly said that 'the offices that surrounded the studio tower were said to be straightforward rooms which need not detain us. ... The office spaces in BH are neither too high nor too low, without ornament but with an air of efficiency which one expects today but which was hardly to be found five years ago'. The general office (or 'G.O.') on the first floor was sparsely decorated and packed with about forty typists. The atmosphere in 1937 was said to be one of 'happy efficiency'.

About fifteen talks came into the office each day (one typist was reckoned to be able to get through three of them at around 7200 words), and were forwarded to 'university trained' girls for checking. By 1938 there were 691 women in the BBC's London offices. They were granted an early-morning break for coffee (work permitting). Afternoon tea was served at their desks, with the girls taking turns to 'pour out'. Staff turnover was relatively low, and apart from those leaving to get married, the number of resignations was said to be 'negligible'. Thanks to the sound-absorbent tiles on the ceiling the relentless clatter of

typewriters was suppressed, to a point, and 'complaints of bad light or faulty ventilation were few'.

A matron's office and clerical school were situated on the same floor. With the vast population in the building, the matron was kept busy. In one year alone she gave 4545 treatments – 2518 to women and 2027 to men – although by 1938 the stretcher had been used only once. The young delivery boys were provided with free fresh milk, and a doctor attended a regular surgery to offer staff inoculations against colds.

The council chamber The council chamber sat above the reception area. Its acoustic qualities were said to be 'strangely happy' to the naked ear, owing to its semicircular shape and simple panelling of Tasmanian oak. At night the room was illuminated with reflected light from lamps concealed in wrought-oak urns. The Queensland walnut tables were designed by McGrath to follow the curve of the walls. The carpet was woven from a heavy cloth stippled with taupe and powder-blue. Complementary curtains were in 'Chelsea stripe', a heavy cotton fabric manufactured by Old Glamis Fabrics and also used in the concert hall green room (see page 85). The fireplace on the right was one of only two in Broadcasting House (the other was in Reith's office; see pages 70–71).

Ground floor

The entrance hall Visitors gained their first impression of Broadcasting House from the reception area. It was designed by Val Myer himself, and was described in the BBC souvenir guide to the building as being 'impressive for the grace of its natural curves, which arise from its semicircular form, and [for] the rhythm of its vertical lines'. The walls were lined with 'English marble', or, more accurately, Hopton-Wood stone. It was a calm, almost spiritual space, with Eric Gill's sculpture *The Sower* occupying the altar position on axis with the front doors. The

inscription below, '*Deus incrementum dat*', translates as 'God giveth the increase' (Corinthians 3:7).

Above the sculpted figure is another Latin inscription, which translates as:

This temple of the arts and muses is dedicated to Almighty God by the first Governors of Broadcasting in the year 1931, Sir John Reith being Director-General. It is their prayer that good seed sown may bring forth a good harvest, that all things hostile to peace or purity may be banished from this house, and that the people, inclining their ear to whatsoever things are beautiful and honest and of good

report, may tread the path of wisdom and uprightness.

Reith later wrote of this dedication that 'there was publicity, much of it probably sarcastic, about the dedication *Deo Omnipotenti* from Philippians 4:8 … it was [BBC Governor] Rendall's composition; the inclusion of my name was his doing. The sentiment was magnificent; I entirely approved of it; but was not sure if the BBC could live up to it.' He later asked Tudsbery if his name could be removed from the inscription.

The reception desk (opposite left) was positioned between the stone columns, in the space between the

limits of Val Myer's ideal semicircular shape (defined by the columns) and the less ideal shape of the site. Next to the desk was a book stall, which sold various BBC publications, and on the other side of the space was an information desk. Visitors could also buy tickets for the Proms, which were held at the Queen's Hall, next door.

The artists' foyer Artists were initially separated from the BBC staff, to 'avoid unnecessary chatting and interference'. This segregated arrangement was short-lived, however, and most people quickly chose the entrance closest to their studio. Opposite the lifts, studio notification boards showed the day's output, including national and regional programmes, and gave a comprehensive timetable for the rehearsals taking place in the studios that day. The boards were protected by glass cases, and used the 'Betterway' signage system, which could also be found at Bush House, Unilever House and Adelaide House. The scale of the operation at Broadcasting House could be seen on a busy day's schedule – sixty-five transmissions and fifty-three rehearsals and balance tests – which might average around 250 hours of activity. The task of allocating the twenty-two studios to the different departments was given to Mr Munroe, the Studio Executive. According to the Post Office film *BBC: The Voice of Britain* of 1934, it was 'the worst job in the building'.

The space by the lifts also contained a post box, a stamp machine and six telephone boxes. A dark internal staircase led from the lobby and was lit by artificial daylight, which was introduced by illuminating false windows on each landing.

Lower ground floor

The concert hall Later called the radio theatre, this room, according to Professor Reilly, was 'the finest thing in the building'. 'Without reliance on traditional forms it yet has great scale and power … altogether it is such a Hall [as] Piranesi might have designed had he dreamed of such instead of prisons.' The first public concerts held in the concert hall were a series of seven chamber music recitals, the first of which was given by the Caterall Quartet on 15 October 1932 (above).

Designed by Val Myer as a venue for classical music, the concert hall was in effect a large studio, and could seat around 550 people, although estimates of its capacity vary somewhat. Unlike in many concert halls, most of the floor space was taken up by the orchestra. The strongly marked piers and beams were intended to express the fact that the room is situated at the heart of the building, and to represent the immensely heavy load of the studios above. False pilasters cleverly housed the hoisting gear for supporting microphones. The brick-and-pumice-concrete walls were covered in a special acoustic plaster, with decorative grooves and coffers to break up the sound waves and reduce echo. The main acoustic benefit of the theatre was an increased 'liveliness and brightness', although artificial reverberation was occasionally used. The diffused lighting at the edges of the space was achieved by Art Deco lenses on top of dado oak panelling at the perimeter of the room.

The panelling was decorated with a series of inset bas-reliefs by the sculptor Gilbert Bayes (1872–1953). The carvings include scenes from Greek mythology and represent Pegasus unsealing the 'Spring of Poetry'; 'Dance, and Provençal song, and sunburnt mirth' (from Keats's 'Ode to a Nightingale'); Odysseus watching Nausicaa and her companions at a game of ball;

'Who are these coming to the sacrifice?' (from Keats's 'Ode on a Grecian Urn'); Milanion conquering Atlanta in the foot-race; and 'Naught so stockish hard and full of rage,/ But music for the time doth change his nature' (from Shakespeare's *The Merchant of Venice*).

In June 1933 the first organ in the country to be designed specifically for microphone transmission was installed. It was equipped with 2362 pipes and had 150 stops, which lit up when activated. The organ was hidden at the far end of the hall behind a bronze grille, which was originally brightly decorated with the BBC crest, although within a year this had

been painted over. The first resident organist was Reginald Foort, and a special broadcast 'opening the organ' was organized, when listeners heard pieces by Bach, Liszt and Handel.

The green room This space was for the artists using the concert hall. It had a chocolate-brown carpet and walls covered in pale green 'Mowear', which was made from South African mohair yarns. 'Chelsea stripe' was used for the curtains. A horizontal mirror covered half of one wall, and, opposite, a wall of black glass interrupted the pink-and-green colour scheme to create the illusion of space. It was complemented by a clock with white-spotted figures and gold feather-shaped hands, mounted on a black glass background.

Basement

Echo rooms There were five rooms in Broadcasting House for making echo sound effects. Sound from a studio was sent to and played in one of the echo rooms on the Portland Place side of the basement (above, top left). A microphone in the echo room picked up the reverberant sound and sent it back to the control room, where the degree of echo could be manipulated.

Listening-rooms There were nine listening-rooms, or 'listening halls', in the building. The two large listening-rooms in the basement were for the use of producers, members of musical staff, press critics or others who needed to hear a transmission under ideal acoustic conditions. Listening-room no. 1 featured a seascape painting by the artist Eastland Fortey, and no. 2 was stunningly decorated in gold and silver foil by McGrath. The gramophone players (as elsewhere in the building) were beautifully made in laminated mahogany – most of them veneered with an ebonized finish – and fitted with gun-metal handles.

In some of the smaller studio listening-rooms, a glass window allowed a view of the performers (above, bottom left). The spaces were acoustically treated to resemble the acoustics of a typical sitting-room, re-creating the conditions in which listeners would receive the programmes. More listening-rooms were later provided on the seventh floor, where the musicians could control and hear the outgoing programmes on loudspeakers without having to sit in the main control room. By 1938 listening-room no. 2 was also being used as a television viewing room and receiving pictures from the BBC's Alexandra Palace studios.

The restaurant Below ground, broadcasting and staff spaces were mixed together. All around were reminders that this was a 'sound factory', with signs that read 'Quiet must be observed in the vicinity of this echo room' and 'Silence is requested from the users of the Listening Hall.'

Nowhere could the excitement and buzzing activity that characterized life in Broadcasting House be seen more clearly than in the McGrath-designed restaurant, which quickly became the social hub of the building. The space was soon operating at all hours of the day and, from the end of December 1932, the night, as the new Empire Service programmes ran into the early hours of the morning. Early informal photographs show a wonderful mixture of staff, visitors and performers taking a meal during a precious interval. In the early 1930s the hard-working catering staff were serving around 6000 lunches a month, but towards the end of the decade an expanded team of 86 staff and 10 chefs was preparing 15,000 lunches, 8000 dinners, 2000 night-time meals, 22,000 morning refreshments and 30,000 afternoon teas every month.

Soon after the building opened, illuminated columns were installed in the restaurant. These lit up to warn artists that they were needed, helping to draw gossiping staff and artists away from their McGrath-designed tables and chairs. A three-course lunch could be bought for sixpence, and, for a penny a day, staff and performers could have Indian or China tea (with biscuits or, on Fridays, a portion of Fuller's cake) served from the McGrath-designed trolleys. A catering manager in 1938 noted the preferences of the different customers: 'The Symphony Orchestra enjoyed tomatoes and lettuce, but the dance band preferred roast beef and Yorkshire pudding.' Comedians, apparently, 'took what was going'. The success of a performance also affected appetites. If a rehearsal had gone well, rump steak and chips was 'a perennial favourite, but if it had gone poorly, salads were preferred'. Contrary, perhaps, to the desires of some of the staff, the restaurant was not licensed to sell alcohol.

Basement and sub-basement

Studio BA: Vaudeville studio

As the building opened, the finishing touches were being put to the studios at the very bottom of the tower. The large 'double-decker', double-height vaudeville studio was used as a miniature theatre and mainly for variety (vaudeville, comedy and revue) performances. There was a stage, floodlighting, a grand piano and space for an audience of sixty.

McGrath was described by Wellesley as a 'magician with colours'. The audience was seated on chromium-plated tubular-metal seats, which were covered with an orange worsted fabric shot with fawn cotton in a basket-weave pattern. The walls were covered with a grey-and-tangerine-coloured fabric woven from polished flax, accented by lemon-yellow, grey-blue and pale-red stripes. The drab matt wall board was transformed into mushroom pink by the silky reflected glow of the colours of the rubber Beatl and lighting. The doors were made from solid teak and lined with yellow Beatl resin sheets, and their edges were covered in rubber to reduce noise on closing. Temporary folding screens covered in yellow-and-black Beatl were used to save space, and provided wings when necessary.

The women's dressing-room
The performers in the small
women's dressing-room were
reflected in black-glass mirrors,
giving an extraordinary illusion
of space. The ceiling was covered
with Lincrusta wallpaper, the silky,
textured surface of which caught
the light wonderfully.

**Studio BB: Dance (jazz) band
studio** The dark-blue door to the
double-height dance band studio
was surrounded by drab wall board
enlivened by 1-inch-wide (2.5 cm)
bright-blue joints. The room had a
balcony for a small audience, with
brushed-copper handrails and a
fascia covered in a reflective black
synthetic resin. The balcony walls
were covered in a flax cloth of fawn,
orange and blue, with a dado of 'high
lavender' mottled with red and black
stripes. The whole design seemed to
echo the sinuous and glossy curves
of the piano – almost as though the
instrument had been turned into a
piece of architecture. Studio BB was

appropriated almost immediately for
television use, and, after providing
the opening broadcast from studio
8A, Henry Hall's newly formed
dance band went to Savoy Hill for
two months, eventually settling
down in the *Children's Hour* studio
upstairs instead.

AIR FOR THE B.B.C.'s NEW "AIR-TIGHT" HOME.

Drawn by our Special Artist, G. H. Davis, from Information Supplied by the Carrier Engineering Company, Ltd., Westminster, London, S.W.1

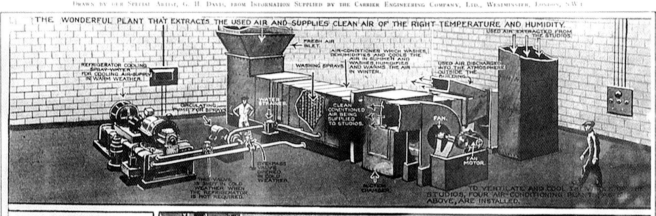

THE WONDERFUL PLANT THAT EXTRACTS THE USED AIR AND SUPPLIES CLEAN AIR OF THE RIGHT TEMPERATURE AND HUMIDITY.

THERMOSTAT FOR AUTOMATICALLY REGULATING AND CONTROLLING AIR SUPPLY AND TEMPERATURE — AS INSTALLED IN EACH STUDIO.

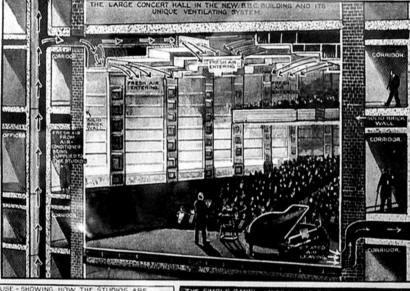

THE LARGE CONCERT HALL IN THE NEW B.B.C. BUILDING AND ITS UNIQUE VENTILATING SYSTEM.

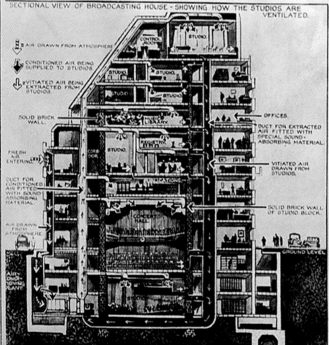

SECTIONAL VIEW OF BROADCASTING HOUSE - SHOWING HOW THE STUDIOS ARE VENTILATED.

THE SIMPLE PANEL CONTROLLING THE VENTILATING SYSTEM OF THE STUDIOS.

"GIVE IT BREATH . . . AND IT WILL DISCOURSE MOST EXCELLENT MUSIC"! THE SCIENTIFIC VENTILATION OF HERMETICALLY SEALED STUDIOS AT THE NEW BROADCASTING HOUSE.

The plant room One of the most impressive features of Broadcasting House was its unique and elaborate system of ventilation. As the studio tower was surrounded entirely by the offices, the studios needed to be provided with fresh air. This caused the designers some problems, as the amount of moisture given off in twelve hours by people in the tower when it was fully occupied was calculated to be 1 ton. Some 180 rooms needed to be supplied, silently, with about 260 tons of fresh air per hour. Allowing for up to 1700 people in the tower, an elaborate automatic temperature-control system was installed in each studio. The Carrier Engineering Company had submitted the highest quotation for the installation, but it was able to give an unequivocal assurance that it could meet the rigorous specification laid down for the studios. Tudsbery went on to write a long report, even offering his resignation if the tender was not accepted. On 24 December 1929, at a meeting with Sir John Reith, Tudsbery was successful in ensuring that the company was appointed.

The proposed system required a relaxation of the by-laws stipulating ventilation to the outside air, and, if designed incorrectly, might have allowed sound to travel from studio to studio. The problem was partly solved by using sound-absorbent material in the air ducts, and by providing four separate air-conditioning plants. In many cases the ducting had to be lengthened so that sufficient sound insulation could be provided. The weight of the building's ducting alone was 120 tons, and three people could walk side by side in the largest pipes. The air was sucked through ventilation slats outside the building by fans and drawn over specially designed water sprays that washed out all particles of dust and soot. There were 32 fans handling 614 tons of air per hour, 16 pumps delivering 641 tons of water per hour, and 54 electric motors with a combined capacity of 504 horsepower. A refrigerator was installed for cooling the studio air in hot weather, and was said to be capable of freezing 200 tons of water per day. The average daily consumption of water in Broadcasting House was around 193,000 gallons (more than 877,000 litres), and the building used an average of 5300 units of electricity every day.

Underneath the restaurant was the boiler room. The capacity of the oil storage tanks was 60 tons, and about 2 tons of oil were used for heating daily. The warm basement made a comfortable home for three cats that had been left behind by the building contractors on the completion of Broadcasting House, and miaowing could occasionally be heard through the ductwork.

Early television in studio BB

While the workmen building the basement of Broadcasting House were wading around in the sticky London clay, something extraordinary was happening less than a mile away. Using existing radio transmitters, the Baird Television Company made Britain's first television broadcast from its Long Acre studio on 30 September 1929, with simultaneous transmission of sound and pictures on 30 March 1930. Soon after Broadcasting House opened, the Baird company installed television equipment in studio BB. On 22 August 1932, after a two-month break in transmission to allow it to take control of both transmission and programme production, the BBC began a regular low-definition thirty-line television service. Transmissions lasted just thirty minutes, and were made four times a week at around 11 pm and midnight, after main radio transmissions had completed, because two wavelengths were needed for sound and vision. Programmes were live, and used a mirror-drum camera that projected a very bright light at the performer from behind a hole in the wall. As the camera was fixed to a tripod, it could be moved only from side to side.

In his book *My Story of the BBC* of 1959, Freddie Grisewood recalled his interview with the tennis star Fred Perry: 'Perry was so nonplussed by the overpowering light that I experienced the greatest difficulty in getting him to concentrate on the matter in hand. Entirely ignoring my questions, ignoring too the unfortunate viewers who had stayed up beyond their bedtime to see him, he blinked incessantly, shaded his eyes, and rambled on: "I say, this light is terrible. You'll really have to do something about it. I'm so dazzled I can't even think."'

During the next few months various weird and wonderful acts were tried out in that bright light. Early TV stars stood in front of a white sheet, on a floor with large black-and-white squares. A wonderful series of photographs in the BBC archive shows animals, various forms of dancing, jugglers, acrobats, cyclists, roller-skating, puppets, shadowgraphs, a Christmas pantomime and a boxing contest. Topical items included Jim Mollison, who had just made the first westward solo flight over the Atlantic, and a seal playing the saxophone. Because the resolution of the screen was low, performers looked rather frightening, with white-painted faces, black noses and purple lips. Other early footage shows the Paramount Astoria Girls dancers in April 1933, dancing about 20 feet (6 m) away from the camera.

Although the girls were allowed a sideways movement of 12 feet (3.5 m), just their heads and shoulders were in shot. In all, there were 76 television transmissions in 1932, and 208 the following year. In 1933 viewers were asked: 'The BBC is most anxious to know the number of people who are actually seeing this television programme. Will those who are looking in send a postcard marked "Z" to Broadcasting House immediately?'

These programmes continued from studio BB until 16 February 1934, when a ten-day interruption in broadcasts allowed a move to a new and larger studio nearby at 16 Portland Place.

HIGHGATE
HILL

LONDON
6 MILES

1936

6 January The BBC purchases the freehold of Broadcasting House.
22 July The BBC Board approves the appointment of architects to design an extension to Broadcasting House.

1938

5 January *Band Waggon* begins, a popular comedy programme set in Broadcasting House.
30 June Resignation of the first Director-General, John Reith.
9 December A BBC press release announces the construction of the extension, to form 'London's New Radio City'.

1939

13 March Princess Elizabeth tours Broadcasting House with King George VI, Queen Elizabeth and Princess Margaret.

1940

18 June General de Gaulle speaks from Broadcasting House after escaping from Nazi-occupied France.
15 October A bomb explodes inside Broadcasting House, killing seven people. The BBC places the order to camouflage Broadcasting House externally.
8 December A landmine explodes on Portland Place, causing fires inside Broadcasting House.

1941

16–17 April Broadcasting House suffers further damage from bombs falling in nearby streets.

1945

8 May Victory in Europe Day. Broadcasting House is hung with flags and floodlit for the first time in eight years.

Broadcasting House Comes of Age

The ever widening sphere of entertainment and of information that broadcasting brings within the reach of every home cannot fail to enrich existence with a store of new interests and of new knowledge, which will surely be reflected in a fuller and happier life, and in a better capacity to meet and face its problems.
BBC Yearbook 1934

Growing pains

Broadcasting House had been open only a few months when Eric Gill's sculpture of Prospero and Ariel above the main entrance began to cause some embarrassment. Ariel's 'organ' was thought to be rather on the large side, and, according to the *Daily Herald* of 23 March 1933, 'maidens are said to blush and youths to pass disparaging remarks regarding the statues of Prospero and Ariel'. Gill was unrepentant. In a newspaper interview he produced the original orders from the BBC committee that had commissioned the statue. According to Gill, the orders clearly stated that 'Ariel should be nude; Prospero was to have a flowing garment.' 'I am only a servant of the BBC,' Gill self-righteously explained, 'and if a statue is passed under the responsibility of Sir John Reith and other directors then it must be all right … supposing I want[ed] to erect an immoral statue outside Broadcasting House, I could not do so. Ariel, the boy, is only ten years old. He cannot be offending women, and are men going to be offended? – I think not.'

However, a local MP, George Gibson Mitcheson, was unfortunate enough to be confronted by the offending appendage every day on his way to and from his house. In the *Evening News* of 23 March 1933 it was reported that he had told Parliament that the figures of Prospero and Ariel were 'objectionable to public morals and decency' and asked the home secretary to instruct the police to compel the BBC to remove Ariel. Despite Gill's protestations, he was eventually forced to compromise, but he left behind a memento of his controversial time working for the BBC. A headline from the *Evening News* of 1 February 1933 revealed the 'Broadcasting House girl that nobody can see – she's made of stone'. Eric Gill is quoted as saying: 'At the back, where nobody can see, is the head of a girl … it was such a pretty girl that I carved it in. Nobody will find it until Broadcasting House falls down.' Gill's prediction, however, was to be proved wrong, and the girl was discovered when the building was cleaned (see page 134).

The problem with Ariel was relatively small compared with Reith's other difficulties. The 'Big House' was not big

enough. During the weeks following the royal opening of Broadcasting House, small changes to the careful designs were already being made, and over the following months staff had to move into nearby houses and further afield. Buildings along Portland Place were acquired, St George's Hall was taken over in 1933 (a year when Reith had to arrange a major reorganization of staff) and new studios were built in Maida Vale in 1934. During the four years following the opening of Broadcasting House, the total number of BBC employees more than doubled; by 1938, there would be nearly 1500 people working there and perhaps another 500 in surrounding offices. By 1936, when the BBC purchased Broadcasting House for £650,000, it had already received nearly three-quarters of a million visitors.

Although licence-payers could still listen to such arcane amusements as the 'BBC versus the listeners' chess match, demand for light entertainment was growing. In the early 1930s Sunday programmes on the BBC remained particularly 'heavy', with serious music forming the main part of the broadcast. These were, according to the newly appointed Director of Variety, Eric Maschwitz, 'as darkly entertaining as a damp Sabbath in a lowland village'. More listeners were tuning into Radio Normandie and Radio Luxembourg, which provided lighter entertainment in a racier American style and, on an evening of dull programming by the BBC, could lay claim to 80 per cent of the audience. Although Sundays remained the same for the time being, the amount of light entertainment was increased to include different bands on other nights of the week. As the BBC settled into its new home, it gradually began to generate its own writers, formats and

Opposite The embarrassment caused by Gill's sculpture was one of Reith's first difficulties as the BBC settled into Broadcasting House. Gill was nearly a year late completing his main figures of Prospero and Ariel, which were eventually finished in the winter of 1932–33. After being winched into position, Prospero was found to be too tall for his niche, and had to have the top of his head trimmed. An article in the *Reynolds News* of 12 February 1933 reported that Gill had been told by the BBC that he 'really must get on'. The article stated: 'Authority at the BBC is pained at the impish glee with which the great sculptor has spun out, entirely at his own expense, the completion of his fascinating task in Portland Place.'

Above Sir John Reith, pictured in the new Broadcasting House. His extraordinary achievements in steering the organization to its new home were beginning to take their toll. He had to organize a significant staff restructuring in 1933, and on 16 November 1935, three years after the move to Broadcasting House, he wrote in his diary: 'I do feel so tired of the BBC.'

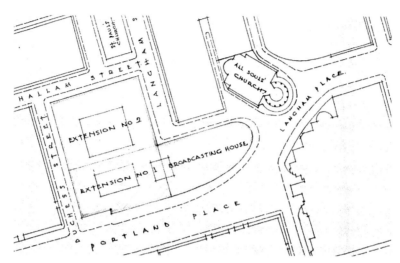

Above, left The BBC soon began to acquire nearby buildings on Langham and Duchess streets and Portland Place. Only a few months after the organization had moved into Broadcasting House, plans were already being made for a substantial new extension. The site plan shows the two proposed northern extensions, which would eventually replace the Georgian terraced houses on the eastern side of Portland Place.

Above, right Georgian houses on the site of the proposed first extension. Number 10 Portland Place, which adjoined Broadcasting House, was occupied by an elderly lady who only moved out under protest, and number 12 was used by the Central Council for Schools Broadcasting. Number 14 was the home of the *Radio Times*. The main entrance of the extension led to a warren of passages and stairs giving access to the Outside Broadcast department, the Empire Service announcer's accommodation (complete with sleeping quarters) and the *Children's Hour* office.

performers. In October 1936 the BBC Listener Research Section was formed. Radio personalities and film stars began to enter through Val Myer's large, heavy doors.

Reith's BBC was changing. He had wanted to get to know all his members of staff personally, but the expansion of the organization and the warren-like environment of Broadcasting House made this difficult for him. It was hard for his staff to share common goals, and difficult to continue the informal communication and pattern of staff relations of Savoy Hill. There was, according to John Cain's book *The BBC: 70 Years of Broadcasting* (1992), 'a small vocal groundswell for less "paternal" goodwill and more "brotherly" goodwill'. Although Reith saw Broadcasting House as 'a great improvement on the improvisations and shortcomings' of their previous headquarters, he would later write: 'I was not happy about the new Broadcasting House, but had not urged my own view against that of others. It was really too early to contemplate a comprehensive headquarters for British Broadcasting, and I did not like the building.' Perhaps he disliked the increased size, professionalism and bureaucracy that it now represented: by 1938 a new member of staff was confronted with the prospect of more than 1700 official BBC forms. Reith himself departed in June of that year, causing the *New Statesman* to ask: 'Breathes there a being fit to sway/ Reith's self-made Empire of the Air?/ The Talking Mongoose is, they say,/ Less rare.'

In spite of all Tudsbery and Val Myer's careful efforts, there were many complaints about the building from BBC staff. The *Architectural Review* of August 1932 had commented on the 'labyrinthine pokiness of the interior', and staff often moaned

about the long and narrow offices. Just a few weeks after the initial move from Savoy Hill there was only one spare office left, which meant that a number of the already poky rooms in the building had to be divided to make more space. Despite the wonderful designs intended to inspire creativity, some studios were also thought to be too small, and some rooms the wrong colour. Many missed the friendly, cosy atmosphere of Savoy Hill. The cramped and, to a certain extent, ad hoc arrangements there had meant that staff were used to improvising and getting along with each other, and had necessitated personal contact and inter-departmental relationships. A certain nostalgia for the early days of the organization had probably already crept in by this stage, but it was nevertheless true that a person could work in one BBC department without ever really needing to meet anyone from any other. Working in a building the size of Broadcasting House could carry with it a certain anonymity.

Worse still, noises could be heard between studios, and the Bakerloo line rumbled below the basement. Early newsreader Freddie Grisewood recalled: 'The supposedly soundproof studios proved to be nothing of the sort. On the contrary the network of air conditioning plant, while serving [its] specific purpose enough, seemed to carry sound all over the building.' There was inadequate lighting for reading scripts and scores, and some doors were too narrow to allow pianos through. Inside the tight confines of the tower, instruments, music stands and the conductor's rostrum had to be carried regularly from the rehearsal rooms in the basement to the military band studio on the top floor. Working for hours and hours in windowless, artificially ventilated spaces could also

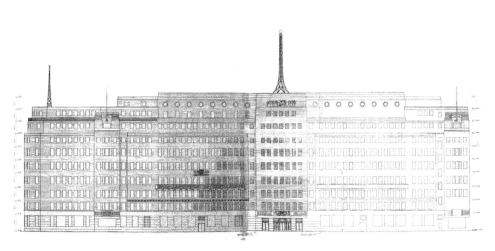

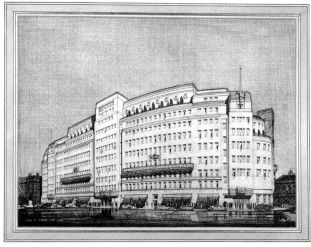

take its toll. In Colin Reid's *Action Stations: A History of Broadcasting House*, Lionel Salter (a producer of music programmes) recalled a studio manager who would put his feet up on the console and immerse himself in *The Times*. Salter had his own way of attracting the manager's attention: 'In the studio I kept a mound of rubbers, which I would hurl at the window every time I wanted to put a disc on.'

Problems also began to emerge in the concert hall. The organ could be heard in other studios as far up as the fourth floor and, in retaliation, big bands playing in the sub-basement could be heard during recitals in the concert hall. A memo from a programme organizer to the studio allocation department on 16 February 1933 read: 'I understand that on Monday last the second half of the chamber music concert in the Concert Hall was badly interfered with by Jack Payne's band in studio BA. We cannot expect people to pay high prices for seats at the chamber concerts, and when they get here give them a mixture of chamber music and dance music.' To make matters worse, a full orchestra could not fit on to the stage. This meant that the front rows of seats would have to be removed, or that concerts would have to be confined to smaller orchestras and recitals. This prompted Grisewood to comment later that 'the Concert Hall was so hopelessly inadequate that in fact, it could only be used for chamber music'. Less than two years after the building opened, the orchestra was moved to new accommodation at Maida Vale.

In an attempt to solve the BBC's space problems, Tudsbery was making plans for two extensions to Broadcasting House. As early as February 1933, in an internal memo, he had discussed the additional studios required in the new building. In May 1938 it was announced that Val Myer, Watson-Hart and Messrs Wimperis, Simpson & Guthrie had been appointed to design the first extension to the north of the building. The *BBC Yearbook 1938* showed a perspective drawing (above, right) that was intended to make the extended Broadcasting House look like one vast new building. The new complex was described in a public announcement as London's 'New Radio City'. Five underground studios were proposed, along with rehearsal rooms, three dramatic studios, effects studios, a large general-purpose studio and, on the eighth floor, a 300-cover restaurant. In a sign of the times, air-raid precautions were included in the design, with the general-purpose studio designated a 'refuge' for staff. A BBC press release stated: 'The architectural treatment of the extension will continue and amplify that of the existing façade to Portland Place, the two portions of the building forming a complete architectural entity that will be both dignified and in harmony with its surroundings.' *The Star* newspaper of 23 August 1939 called it 'one of the finest buildings of its kind in the world'. On 27 July 1938 it was announced by the BBC that the houses at 10–22 Portland Place were being cleared in readiness for the extension to Broadcasting House. In the 'Microphone' section of the *Radio Times* dated 26 August 1938, readers were informed that 'at last demolition of Portland Place (No.'s 10–22) has begun.' But these plans were to be short-lived.

Above, left An early drawing of the proposed extension, showing a more-or-less symmetrical elevation to Portland Place, with a larger, central entrance to the concert hall. The extension is effectively a mirror image of Broadcasting House.

Above, right A perspective of the preferred scheme, showing its symmetrical nature. In all, five schemes were submitted to the Royal Fine Art Commission for approval. Adjustments were made to take the commission's views into account, and as a result the ninth floor was lost.

The Woodrooffe incident

Reith's early problems were difficult enough, but there were two particular events that would eventually prove fatal to the carefully planned arrangement of the studios in the tower. On 20 January 1936 the broadcast of a rather upbeat Henry Hall Dance Band concert from a Maida Vale studio resumed following the announcement that King George V was seriously ill (he died later that day). This was embarrassing, but just over a year later, on 20 May 1937, Lieutenant-Commander Thomas Woodrooffe's outside broadcast from the coronation celebrations at the Spithead Review continued despite the fact that he was obviously inebriated. Woodrooffe (opposite, top) had been sent to HMS *Nelson* to 'pick up some atmosphere' and had run into some old Navy friends. Returning to the microphone some time later in a rather over-confident manner, he soon revealed that he had soaked up a little too much of that atmosphere:

At the present moment, the whole fleet is lit up. When I say 'lit up', I mean lit up by fairy lamps. We've forgotten the whole Royal Review … we've forgotten the Royal Review … the whole thing is lit up by fairy lamps. It's fantastic; it isn't the fleet at all. It's just … it's fairyland, the whole fleet is in fairyland. Now, if you'll follow me through … if you don't mind … the next few moments … you'll find the fleet doing odd things. At the present moment, the New York, obviously, is lit out … and when I say the fleet is lit up … in lamps … I mean, she's outlined. The whole ship's outlined. In little lamps. … I'm sorry, I was telling some people to shut up talking. Umm … what I mean is this. The whole fleet is lit up. In fairy lamps, and … each ship is outlined. … In a second or two, we're going to fire rockets, um, we're going to fire all sorts of things [indistinct]. And … you can't possibly see them, but you'll hear them going off, and you may hear my reaction when I see them go off. Because … erm … I'm going to try and tell you what they look like as they go off. But at the moment there's a whole huge fleet here. The thing we saw this afternoon, this colossal fleet, lit up … by lights … and the whole fleet is in fairyland! It isn't true, it isn't here! … It's gone! It's gone! There's no fleet! It's, eh, it's disappeared! No magician who ever could have waved his wand could have waved it with more acumen than he has now at the present moment. The fleet's gone. It's disappeared. … There's nothing between us and heaven. There's nothing at all.

Woodrooffe was oblivious to his increasingly desperate engineer's attempts to stop him from speaking, but was eventually cut off. Attempts to ensure that no more damage was done were further frustrated when he managed to escape from his cabin (in which he had been discreetly locked) and was later found 'enjoying himself in the officers' mess'. Rather surprisingly, the convivial commentator was suspended for only a week, and went on to commentate for the BBC on other occasions, including the 1938 FA Cup Final between Preston and Huddersfield. Here he famously declared that, should a goal be scored in the last minute of extra time, he would eat his hat. Unfortunately for Woodrooffe, Preston scored from a penalty.

New methods of controlling programmes

It became obvious that, in order to prevent such incidents happening in the future, a duty announcer was required to be closer to the control engineer, so that immediate decisions could be made. In the two or three years before the outbreak of war, as technical equipment became more compact and new switching systems were developed, there was a growing feeling that the original methods of operation in Broadcasting House were fundamentally wrong.

It was decided that the technical and operational control of programmes should be transferred from the control room to a series of small rooms that would eventually become known as 'continuity suites'. The pairing of a studio control cubicle with an adjacent studio allowed the spaces to be used for rehearsal and transmission, and – with more compact technical equipment – would enable producers to rehearse their programmes both artistically and technically. The producer would be served by a 'programme engineer', who would be on duty in the cubicle during the rehearsal period and who was responsible for balancing and controlling the programme during transmission. The engineer would select the sources of the programme, fade and mix them as required, and 'maintain aural supervision of the sequence of programmes as a whole': in other words, maintain continuity of the output.

The continuity desk in the cubicle allowed the engineer to continue transmitting the studio output while preparing the announcement studio for transmission and listening to the incoming outside broadcast. The adjoining studio enabled announcements (such as the starting and finishing of outside broadcasts) to be made without needing to book a special studio for the purpose. Gramophone 'fill-ups' could also be played from the studio, and emergency announcements could be made at short notice.

The BBC *Engineering Training Manual* of 1942 summed up the changes:

There was a tendency in peacetime for broadcasts to become technically over-elaborate .... With the introduction of local control and the use of larger studios, this multi-studio tendency has largely disappeared and the engineering problems associated with big productions have correspondingly lessened. In any case, the stringencies of wartime broadcasting make such economies essential both as regards accommodation and equipment.

In 1937 the last of the old type of studio (with its listening-room) had been added in the north-west corner of the fourth floor, but by April of the following year proposals had been made to convert the concert hall and studios BA, BB (the old experimental TV studio), 3A, 3E, 6A and 8A to the new arrangement. Later in 1938, following complaints about the facilities in the third-floor 'talks' studios, it was decided that the paired configuration should become the BBC standard for this type of studio. In 1939 a small emergency London control room was built in a basement room near the gallery of Studio BA, and was used during air raids; it became impossibly cramped, so studio BA was used for this purpose instead. Two continuity suites were also constructed along the western wall of the studio, one for the Home Service and the other for the Forces programme, effectively spelling the end of McGrath's wonderful studio and Coates's control room on the eighth floor.

Wartime programmes

The Second World War brought the BBC its greatest challenge yet, although most listeners would be unaware of the difficulties involved in keeping the radio going. For security and ease of communication, the BBC's regional services were amalgamated into a single station known as the Home Service. At first listeners were fed on a diet of war bulletins, endless government announcements and fussy instructions, interspersed with light music, that earned the Corporation the unaffectionate sobriquet 'Auntie'. The fingers of the BBC theatre organist, Sandy MacPherson, were working overtime. He played no fewer than forty-five programmes featuring 'familiar and well-loved melodies' during the first two weeks of the war. They soon became less-loved melodies, however, as the constant sound of the organ drove many listeners – and people working in the building – to despair. In September

1939, out of Britain's total population of 48 million, the Home Service probably had at least 34 million listeners, but by the beginning of October, 35 per cent of the public were fed up with the BBC and 10 per cent had stopped listening altogether. The press used such words as 'puerile', 'travesty', 'amateurish' and 'a paucity of ideas' to describe the output. Although it was obvious that the BBC was to be a vital cog in the war machine, it was not yet clear how this would work.

Gradually new kinds of programme emerged from the chaos. The news was essential listening, but people also wanted high-quality entertainment and to feel connected to their loved ones. At the beginning of 1940 a station called the BBC Forces Programme was launched for people to dip into, a practice called 'tap listening'. Being mainly light entertainment, it was very different from the BBC's previous output. This lighter touch became popular at home and abroad. *Band Waggon* was first broadcast on 5 January 1938 and starred Arthur Askey and Richard Murdoch, who shared a mythical flat at the top of Broadcasting House, where they were caretakers of the six time-signal pips. Such programmes as *Happidrome, Hi Gang, Garrison Theatre, Workers' Playtime* and Vera Lynn's *Sincerely Yours* (dismissed by the BBC Governors as 'popularity noted but deplored') kept up the nation's morale while the country was in the depths of war. MacPherson's fingers were given a rest on 6 September 1939, when Tommy Handley sang 'Who is this man who looks like Charlie Chaplin?' In his surreal comedy *It's That Man Again* (ITMA), Handley played the Minister of Aggravation and Mysteries, who was housed in the Office of Twerps. Other characters included Sir Short Supply, the German spy Funf (who spoke into a glass tumbler), Ali Oop (the saucy postcard vendor) and Mrs Tickle (later to be replaced by Mrs Mopp). By 1944 ITMA had become essential listening, with nearly 16 million people regularly tuning in, and it would run for ten years. In a more serious broadcast, General de Gaulle addressed his countrymen from Broadcasting House in June 1940, following his escape from Nazi-occupied France.

And the music continued. Played on the BBC concert hall organ and broadcast in a twice-daily programme called *Music While You Work*, it was provided to keep wartime workers contented. Not all melodies were deemed suitable, however, and modern slow waltzes were banned completely because of their 'soporific tendencies'. Apparently, one pianist actually fell off his stool and died before the end of a broadcast, and had to be left there until the programme went off air.

Broadcasting House under attack

Last Thursday night's plans for evacuating the children of London gave further proof of how broadcasting can be used to maintain order and guide action.
'Crisis in the Machine Age', The Listener, 6 October 1939

In the last days of August 1939 sandbags appeared outside Broadcasting House. Other precautions had already been taken: two years earlier, gas-proof doors were fitted to all lift shafts and all staircases leading to the basement, bulletproof-steel shutters were added to the ground-floor windows while those around the entrance hall were bricked up, an emergency control room and a telecommunications space were relocated in the basement, and the pavement lights to Langham Street were protected with concrete. The building was painted dark green, on orders to 'tone down external surfaces of Broadcasting House to approved single colour, using "wallgrease", guaranteed … as removable from Portland stone by steam-process without leaving stains'. As war broke out, only a skeleton staff would continue to operate from Broadcasting House, mainly to keep 'talks' and news programmes going. In May 1940 a military guard was posted to protect the building from attack or sabotage by fifth columnists or parachute troops. In July 1940, with the basement work only partly completed, it was decided that work on the extension should stop.

Three months later, at 8.05 on the evening of 15 October 1940, a delayed-action 500-lb (230-kg) German bomb landed in the music library. It lay silent for nearly an hour, and then exploded. Bruce Belfrage, who was reading the nine o'clock news at the time, stopped as he heard the bomb go off. Plaster and dust fell on to his script but, after a slight pause, with someone whispering 'It's all right', he managed to finish reading the bulletin. A few floors above, the bomb had killed seven of his colleagues.

The bomb also caused serious damage to the building, extending from the third to the eighth floors (below). Writing a month later, BBC engineer Tudsbery commented that the upper half of the tower was more seriously shaken than had previously been supposed. The roof was lifted and close inspection of the steel frame that supported it was to be made. The destruction of the west and central tower walls on the fifth floor meant a great deal of shoring up was necessary. It would take three years to restore the studios.

One of the staff, Clare Lawson Dick, described the atmosphere in Broadcasting House at the time:

In the daytime we worked above ground. Then, as the sirens went at dusk, we descended into the basements, three floors of them, … and there we worked and played, ate and drank and slept on the floor on pallets until the daytime. I shall never forget the intensity of that communal life. In those basements you would find freedom fighters from France still in the fisherman's blouses in which they had just rowed across the Channel; elegants like Eve Curie, daughter of Marie Curie; exotics like the coloured singer Elizabeth Welch, trapped there for a while by the raids; secretaries formed into fire-fighting teams; producers, actors, writers, journalists, war correspondents and the

Opposite, left On Wednesday 6 September 1939 the first live revue after the declaration of war featured Tommy Handley singing 'Who is this man who looks like Charlie Chaplin?'

Opposite, right The first few weeks of the Second World War were difficult for the BBC. The Corporation had two alternatives when it came to putting on variety programmes: gramophone recordings or Sandy MacPherson at the BBC organ. As the console was mounted on a dolly and could be placed remotely, MacPherson went on air live from St George's Hall (which was next door to the Queen's Hall) at 4.45 pm on Sunday 3 September 1939, and during the following two weeks he played a staggering forty-five programmes. People wrote to the BBC to say that they would rather face the German guns than hear more of MacPherson.

Far left Broadcasting House took a direct hit from a 500-lb (230-kg) delayed-action bomb on 15 October 1940. The switchboard, news library and thousands of gramophone records were destroyed. At 6 am the following day the news librarian, trying to save some of his files from among the debris in Portland Place, was arrested for looting.

Left Bruce Belfrage continued calmly to read the news after the bomb had exploded.

Top left Most of the staff working in Broadcasting House were moved out of London before war was declared. Those left in the building were engineers, newsroom staff and members of the foreign-language sections. Staff and artists often stayed overnight because air raids made it too dangerous to leave. Clare Lawson Dick (on the top bunk), who had joined the BBC in 1935, recalled her wartime experiences in Broadcasting House.

Top right The attack of 8 December 1940 caused fire damage to much of the building, including the offices and studios. This extraordinary image shows Maufe's religious studio 3E (see pages 74–75) completely burned out, apart from Vernon Hill's icon in the foreground, which survives apparently unscathed.

Bottom left At the outbreak of war police guarded the building day and night. In May 1940 they were replaced by soldiers. Inside, local defence volunteers patrolled the studios and corridors, wearing armbands and carrying truncheons.

Bottom right Staff clear up the fire damage to the offices after the attack of 8 December 1940. Below ground, an emergency control room had been installed in the vaudeville studio, and the newsroom also moved to the basement. By the following morning parts of these floors had also been damaged – not by fire, but by flooding from the firemen's hoses.

Opposite Early in the war it was decided to make the building less conspicuous in moonlight by painting it dark green. Outside the main entrance, an armoured car waits to drive announcers to the Maida Vale studios should transmission from Broadcasting House become impossible.

Overleaf The concert hall was used as a huge dormitory from the very beginning of the war, as it was expected that London would immediately be heavily bombed. Staff sleeping was arranged on a ticket system, and a large curtain towards the back of the hall divided the sexes. This photograph was taken in 1940.

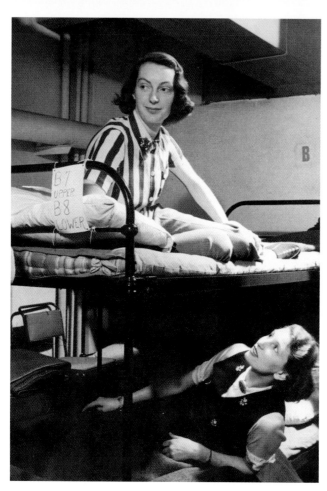

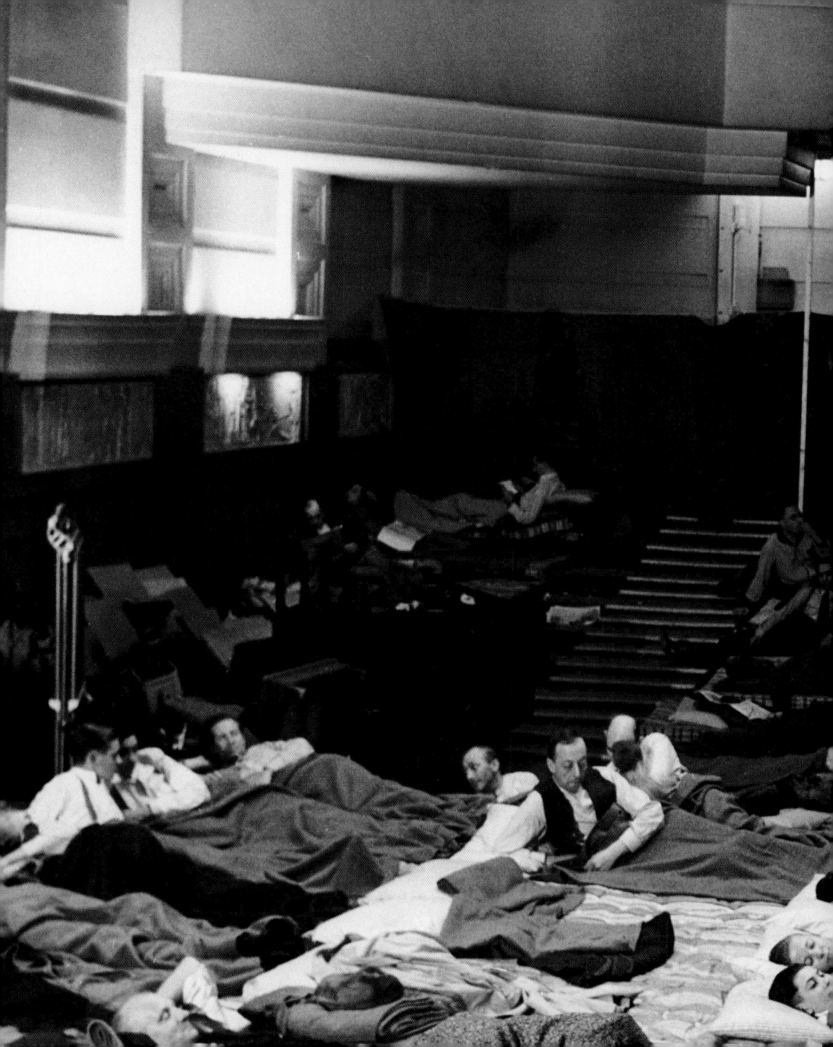

wonderful members of the BBC foreign teams who broadcast to Europe and the world. The Concert Hall in Broadcasting House was turned into a dormitory. The seats had been removed from the auditorium and the staff laid mattresses on the tiered steps, wriggled into sleeping bags made of sheets and drew a rough blanket over all. A washing line, with blankets hung over it, divided the men's section from the girls'. One night Mr Frederick Ogilvie, then Director-General, appeared at the back of the hall and said: 'Will the girls please get down amongst the men as there's a time bomb just behind them in the excavations.' In a second the men were on their feet, dragging on their trousers and generally arranging themselves, whilst we girls whistled down amongst them without waiting for any decencies or courtesies.

Grisewood, in his book *My Story of the BBC* (1959), describes mentioning to a lift attendant the effectiveness of the thin curtain that divided the staff in the concert hall. The attendant replied, 'Oh, I don't know, sir. I don't suppose there'll be much fun and games there – not while there's a war on.' Grisewood suggested the remark could 'lead only to the conclusion that in normal circumstances the place might have become a shambles'.

In Colin Reid's book *Action Stations: A History of Broadcasting House* (1987), Margaret Hubble, a programme assistant for the Empire Service, recalled her wartime experiences:

We had a studio on the fourth floor of the tower. When the sirens went, which was pretty well every night, we gathered all our papers and schedule material and went down to the basement, where we had a small restaurant table, in what was known as the Restaurant Annexe. It was rather cramped to say the least. We had to stay in BH for three days and three nights non-stop. Then we had three days and three nights completely clear to get out of London, if that was possible. Originally, anybody who stayed overnight was sleeping in the Concert Hall. … We found that system of sleeping was bad because we didn't get enough rest, so after a while we were allotted [a studio that] was still in use at night. It was all very difficult because very often there was no light. There were no batteries left for torches in those days, and if you struck a match, it smelled foul because the atmosphere wasn't very good anyway. You couldn't see where you were going, the mattresses being so close together, scattered around the studio, one under the grand piano. We used to put a plan up in the Office with the mattresses drawn on it. You had to put your name on the one you were going to occupy, but it wasn't always foolproof. One night I was the last one left working. I entered the 'dormitory' convinced I was [to sleep] under the

grand piano. I groped my way along, feeling the edge of the mattresses, on which people were sleeping, [and] plonked my hand hard on the one under the piano, where somebody sat bolt upright and said: 'Who's that? Is that you Hubble-bubble?' It was the Overseas Presentation Officer, Duncan Carse. I had to go out again, [to] look at the plan to discover which mattress was unoccupied. Shortly afterwards, Duncan was asked about our sleeping arrangements in BH by Matron, who was responsible for health. He took her in and showed her our studio camp. All the mattresses were piled up high. She was horrified to learn that first of all men and women had been sleeping there together. She was no less horrified when Duncan said to her: 'Well, Matron, if you imagine that anybody has any energy left for anything other than going to sleep by the time we get to bed, you've got another think coming!'

Between 200 and 300 staff were on duty or sleeping when, late on the evening of Sunday 8 December 1940, a landmine went off in Portland Place. The explosion killed twenty-three-year-old PC John Charles Vaughan. A witness, L.D. Macgregor, described the scene: '[There was] a large ball of blinding white light with two concentric rings of colour – the inner one lavender and the outer one violet. The ball, some ten to twenty feet [3–6 m] high, was near to a lamp post. The noise was indescribable, something like a colossal growl – and was accompanied by a veritable tornado of air blast.' Another eyewitness described it as being 'like a scene from Dante's Inferno'. Broadcasting House was on fire for about seven hours, and by morning the lower ground floors, the concert hall and a number of studios were flooded with water. Although the explosion caused damage from the ground floor to the seventh floor, the structure and staff survived relatively unscathed.

Broadcasting House suffered serious damage on one more occasion, when a bomb fell at the corner of nearby Bolsover and New Cavendish streets in the early hours of 17 April 1941. Although the explosion destroyed a number of the surrounding buildings, damage to the offices in Broadcasting House was described as comparatively 'slight', but most of the windows on the east side of the building were blown in and many office doors blown out. It was estimated that the war damage would cost around £50,000 and that it would take a year to repair the structure and three years to restore the studios, although it was hard to be accurate about the detailed cost of reconstruction; the figure was said to be 'a very wild guess indeed'.

In further air raids on 16–17 April 1941 there was more 'serious and spectacular bomb damage' in houses near to Broadcasting House. At 10.12 in the evening a 200-lb (90-kg) bomb fell in Chapel Mews, just behind Langham Street, starting a number of fires and demolishing the BBC's offices in Langham and Wyndham streets, as well as the Devonshire public house. At 2.26 in the morning another bomb fell at the corner of Bolsover and New Cavendish streets, blowing in nearly all the windows on the east side of Broadcasting House.

accommodation for four news studios with cubicles, as well as an adjoining telecommunications room, a control room, a diesel-engine room and toilets. Alterations were made to the design in October 1941, when the floor levels were changed to match the levels of the basement and ground floor of the proposed new extension to Broadcasting House. In the summer of 1942 protection to the roof slab was increased by individually casting 4¾-ton concrete blocks on builder's felt for convenience of breaking-out at a later date. Each block had two lifting eyes to allow removal, when the surface of the slab could become part of the ground floor of the incomplete extension. A simple inscription on the wall leading to the main entrance read 'BBC AD 1942'.

George Orwell described the atmosphere inside Broadcasting House during the war as 'something half way between a girls' school and a lunatic asylum'. But to the outside world, at least, the BBC remained an essentially conservative and reassuring institution. As with the General Strike years earlier, the onset of war had been a key test for the organization. As early as December 1940, a tribute to the BBC staff had been given in the House of Commons, praising their 'endurance, hard work, patriotism and physical courage', and on 3 April 1941 Field Marshal Montgomery had paid a private visit to Broadcasting House. On the night of 8 May 1945, VE (Victory in Europe) Day, Broadcasting House was decorated with flags and floodlit for the first time since the coronation in 1937. The BBC had continued to provide a broadcasting service through times of unparalleled difficulty.

During the months that followed the war, flowers and gifts poured into Broadcasting House, including a tapestry from France, a plaque from Norway and a vase from The Netherlands. Despite its faltering start the BBC had forged strong bonds with its audiences and helped to maintain national unity and morale. The Corporation was now twenty-three years old and had developed into a mature broadcasting organization. But as the BBC emerged into the post-war world, Broadcasting House could no longer remain centre stage.

The 'stronghold'

After the Blitz of 1940–41 it was decided that a safe refuge was necessary. Tudsbery came up with the ambitious idea of getting London Transport to build 'two low level security tunnels' beneath Broadcasting House, to which he planned to provide access via an 80-foot-deep (24 m) shaft. The scheme was never realized, but it survives in the persistent rumour of a secret underground link between Broadcasting House and the Bakerloo line of the London Underground. A more practical solution was adopted, and a heavily reinforced concrete structure built on the north-east corner of Duchess and Hallam streets. The 'stronghold', as it was called, was designed to withstand a direct hit from a 'medium-case high-explosive 500-lb [230-kg] bomb'. It was completely self-contained and sealed against gas attack, and provided

Opposite The 'stronghold' was effectively a miniature broadcasting station built on the site of the proposed extension, and was designed to be used should Broadcasting House be destroyed. It contained studios, a control room and transmitters and would offer complete protection against a direct hit from a 'medium-case' 500-lb (230-kg) bomb. Duchess Street is at the top left of the photograph, and Hallam Street to the right.

Left Field Marshal Montgomery's visit to Broadcasting House. The wire-and-steel anti-blast pillbox at the entrance to the building was constructed after the bombing had begun, and the original sandbag defences augmented with large concrete blocks.

1946

The repair of the principal war-damaged studios in Broadcasting House is completed.

1957–61

Construction of the first extension to Broadcasting House.

1965

The BBC purchases the Langham Hotel.

1972

1 November The Queen visits Broadcasting House and the BBC's Fiftieth Anniversary Exhibition at the Langham Hotel.

1982

The BBC commissions architect Norman Foster to study its accommodation needs. This leads to the design of a new Radio Building on the site of the Langham Hotel. The project is cancelled in 1985.

1990

5 September The BBC decides to focus its development in west London. A new building opens at White City.

1991

BBC architects begin to design a building to fill in the courtyard within the Broadcasting House extension. The new structure is completed in 1995.

1994

The BBC concert hall reopens after refurbishment and is renamed the radio theatre.

1997

20 October The BBC Experience is opened by the Queen.
November–March 1998 The BBC commissions a series of studies into the design of its workspaces. This results in a new open-plan corporate 'floor' being built in Broadcasting House in the spring of 1998.

1998

3 July *Today* is broadcast from Broadcasting House for the last time, as the News department moves to White City.

'Once Breathtaking, Now Comforting'

Right The shrapnel-damaged wall of Broadcasting House in 1941. Cracks in the walls had appeared as early as 1938, and twenty years later Tudsbery wrote that other structural defects had been found, meaning that the war-damaged stone would, after all, need to be replaced.

Opposite After the war the major developments in the world of broadcasting took place outside Broadcasting House. Inside the building it was a story of slow evolution, not revolution, and the interior was remodelled to respond to developments in technology and programming. This included the construction of a new drama studio, 6A, in 1946 (pictured) and alterations to other studios, including the installation of a cubicle in the concert hall in July 1956.

To someone like myself, who has watched the 'spoken word' grow from small beginnings to its present importance, the general trend of the moment is a little disheartening.
Freddie Grisewood, BBC employee, 1959

During the two years after the war, the signs of attack were slowly removed from Broadcasting House and the solid concrete defences taken down. A workman recalled that this took time: 'When we opened up with the first pneumatic drill, there was such a to-do about the noise penetrating to the studios, where broadcasting was going on, that we had to drop it. Now we are back to the old hammer and chisel.' It took a year to remove the protective overcoat by hand. The robust design of Broadcasting House had allowed it to survive the war, but it had been seriously wounded. Outside, the Portland stone cladding was pitted by shrapnel, and despite Tudsbery's original sentiment that the building should proudly retain its scars he had to authorize the replacement of some of the stone when it was discovered that it had been split through. Inside the building things were worse, as many of the floors, walls and ceilings had been lost or rendered unusable by the bombing. The standard of the repair work reflected the difficult circumstances under which it was carried out, and was patchy, to say the least. As early as 1945 nearly all the carefully designed pieces of bespoke furniture, delicate fittings and fragile acoustic wall boards of 1932 had been lost for ever.

The war had seen the number of BBC staff swell from 5100 in 1939 to 11,000 by 1946, but as it ended many of the London staff were scattered between separate buildings. The BBC had first leased part of Bush House in September 1940, and new accommodation was urgently needed for the expanding European services. After being evacuated to a temporary home in Maida Vale, the latter had moved to Bush House early in 1941. In 1945 the BBC began leasing space in the Langham Hotel and occupying the adjacent Egton House (designed in 1938 by Marshall & Tweedy) in Langham Street. Brian Johnston, the BBC's legendary cricket commentator, was one of the new members of staff based outside Broadcasting House. He was quite happy with the situation: 'My first impressions of Broadcasting House weren't that good. I found the atmosphere claustrophobic, while the meetings I had to attend were boring. Senior staff had carpeted offices, but there was no carpet in my office at 55 Portland Place, where several of us used to play indoor

Above, left In 1957, nearly twenty-five years after the initial idea was proposed, Broadcasting House was finally extended. The new building provided much-needed additional space and ensured that Broadcasting House would remain the BBC's radio headquarters.

Above, right, and opposite The preparations made for the Queen's coronation in 1953 represented a shift from the world of radio to that of television. Broadcasting House was decorated to mark the occasion.

cricket to pass the time. If an official telephoned from BH we used to pull his leg, saying: "Would you mind hanging on until we finish the over?"' The film *Close Up* (1949) offers another behind-the-scenes glimpse of the recovering organization at work.

In 1947 the building was washed down to remove the camouflage. During the following few years, the repair of the war damage enabled changes to be made. The new pairs of studios and cubicles replaced the original layouts within the tower itself. A new double-height drama studio (6A) was completed in 1946, studio 8A was refurbished in 1950 and the concert hall received its own cubicle. Attempts were made to improve the acoustic performance of the pre-war studios by increasing the depth of their delicate acoustic linings, as well as faceting or curving the acoustic panels within the spaces to counter acoustic reflections and improve the sound.

But bigger changes were looming. A cable had connected Broadcasting House to Wembley in 1948 for the coverage of the Olympics on television. By the time preparations were being made for the broadcast of the coronation of Elizabeth II in 1953, the radio men were sidelined for the first time. ITV started in 1955, and by the end of the decade the *Radio Times* had reversed the order of its pages, putting television at the front and radio at the back of the magazine. It was clear that the new world wanted pictures, not just words. The flags and flowers that bedecked Broadcasting House for the coronation would herald the new world of pictures, and the remainder of the decade would see a slow decline in the number of people listening to the radio. Between 1951 and 1954 the number of combined sound and television licences doubled to well over

3 million. In 1956 the BBC began to build Television Centre at White City in west London. Television had arrived.

A neighbour for Broadcasting House

The BBC's radio operation remained desperately short of space. A press release issued by the Corporation on 14 December 1955 informed the public that 'the BBC has let the vacant site adjoining Broadcasting House to the Prudential Assurance Co. Ltd., who have agreed to construct an office building which will have a different architectural style, but will be in sympathy with Broadcasting House'. This new building would house administrative facilities and occupy the site of the extension that had been proposed before the war. In addition, the bomb-damaged part of Hallam Street provided more space for expansion, along with that occupied by a further six substantial Georgian houses, which were scheduled to be pulled down (although not without a fight by an elderly lady, Mrs Jane Ellen Hawkins, who steadfastly refused to move). The proposed new H-shaped extension was designed by H. Fitzroy Robinson with Sir Howard Robertson, and roughly matched the height of Broadcasting House. Construction began in February 1957 and was completed in 1961. Plans to house only offices were revised so that the extension also contained eleven new studios, along with a number of smaller recording and editing spaces. The ground- and first-floor areas were used for a new main London control room along with other technical facilities and parking space for sixty BBC vans, mobile transmitters and programme-control vehicles. On the top floor thirsty staff would be provided with BBC tea in

By the late 1960s Broadcasting House seemed to represent an older, more genteel world, and many BBC staff thought the building stuffy. Nowhere could the contrast between the old and the new generations of broadcasters be seen more than in the new Radio 1, which first broadcast from continuity studio 1 on the first floor. It introduced such new talent as Kenny Everett (left), seen larking about in reception in 1970, and Tony Blackburn (right), who was pictured outside a grimy Broadcasting House (it was finally cleaned to celebrate its fiftieth birthday in July 1972).

a new roof-terrace restaurant, with views north as far as Hampstead Heath and south to the Surrey hills.

Navigation around Broadcasting House had never been easy, and the new extension (christened BHX, or Broadcasting House Extension), with hundreds of rooms and with floors at different levels, made it even harder. But with its new facilities and studio spaces, the new building would bring renewed vitality to the BBC's old headquarters. In February 1965, as in 1932, four years after moving into a leasehold property the Governors approved the proposal to purchase the freehold, at a cost of £1.85 million.

The atmosphere in the spacious and light-filled new extension reinforced the contrast with the small, dark rooms of the old Broadcasting House, where it was as if Reith's ghost still lumbered around the building. A year after the purchase of the extension, John Simpson recalled in David Hendy's *Life on Air: A History of Radio Four* how Reith's 'gloomy influence' still pervaded the corridors of Broadcasting House. He described his colleagues in the building as 'tweedy, briefcased, polite, earnest, slightly arty, nonconformist, yet distinctively conformist as well … the newsroom was an island away from the world, not in it'. They inhabited a peaceful Reithian world of quiet studiousness. The comfortable atmosphere of Broadcasting House, with its shut doors and dark corridors, seemed increasingly at odds with the world outside. Simpson wanted to escape as quickly as possible.

The next few years would see major changes for radio services. As the organization approached middle age, it would need to learn to swing. The *BBC Yearbook 1967* described

'a year of challenge and opportunity'. Indeed, 1967 would prove to be a pivotal year for British radio. Four new national radio stations were launched, followed shortly afterwards by a dozen new local radio services, giving listeners an unprecedented choice of programmes. By the end of the 1960s the decline in listeners had been reversed, and twice as many radio sets were bought in the year of the 'summer of love' as in 1958. After years of broadcasting to the world, the BBC was reaching further and deeper into its own country.

The expansion in services came at a cost, however, as there was less money to go round at Broadcasting House. The different departments Reith had wished to unite battled for budgets, with little reason to mix. Soon Radio 1 was celebrating its own first five years of broadcasting on the roof of the building. Tony Blackburn was pictured outside a dirty-looking Broadcasting House, and the young DJ Kenny Everett was photographed in reception, perched on a stepladder in front of the Latin inscription (below).

Despite the investment in new stations, by the late 1970s it looked as though the success of television might spell the end of radio. Some thought multi-channel television could be the beginning of the end, and many working in Broadcasting House believed that radio might not survive into the new millennium. Somewhat prophetically, between 1974 and 1980 an enormous 35-foot-long (10 m) crack appeared in the walls of Broadcasting House. Something radical needed to be done.

A missed opportunity

In 1981 English Heritage awarded Broadcasting House a Grade II listing to reflect its historical and architectural importance. A year later, almost exactly fifty years after Broadcasting House had opened, the BBC commissioned the architect Norman Foster to develop ideas to house its Radio operation in a single state-of-the-art building. After taking over more and more of the Langham Hotel, the BBC had eventually purchased the building in 1965. Foster proposed the demolition of the hotel and the construction of a new headquarters for BBC Radio, but, after three years of intensive work, escalating costs and changes in BBC management, the project was cancelled. This decision disappointed not only the staff but also the wider architectural community. It prompted the *Architectural Review* of May 1987 to lament the loss of 'one of the most elegant and assured new buildings that Londoners have had within their grasp for some time'. Foster would have made an appropriate guest on the BBC's then newly commissioned programme *Loose Ends*.

Instead, the BBC sold the Langham Hotel and decided to focus its London expansion plans on White City in the west of the capital. On 5 September 1990 a new BBC building was opened there. But while it solved an immediate space problem, it lacked architectural ambition, just at the time when other broadcasters were using architecture to symbolize the efficiency of their operations. The completion of the slick Independent Television News headquarters in Gray's Inn Road in 1990 allowed Norman Foster to add a broadcast building to his expanding portfolio, and his

In 1982 Norman Foster proposed a new radio building on the site of the Langham Hotel. The scheme incorporated a public street connecting Langham Place with Cavendish Square. Views of the model show the new building from the porch of All Souls (left); its dominant position on Portland Place (below, right); and the glazed public street (below, left). The longitudinal section (bottom) shows the new building in the context of All Souls Church and Broadcasting House.

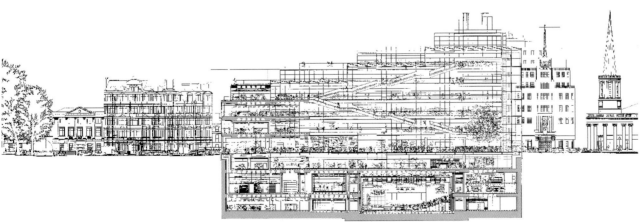

ex-partner, Richard Rogers, completed the new Channel 4 headquarters in Westminster in 1994. Meanwhile the BBC continued to make do with Broadcasting House, and design work was started on a further extension (which was rather pragmatically christened BHXX) to fill in the courtyard behind Broadcasting House.

Val Myer's building, now listed, had been described in 1986, in the *Foster Rogers Stirling* exhibition at the Royal Academy, as 'hopelessly obsolete'. Putting its money into programme-making rather than buildings, the BBC had struggled to maintain its portfolio of around thirty properties in the capital. The less than ideal conditions were accepted by the London staff, including Terry Wogan: 'Endless corridors, basement studios, shuddering to the passing of underground trains, holes in the carpet covered with gaffer tape, air conditioning, cold in winter, hot in summer and controlled from somewhere up north. Twelve years of broadcasting to a brick wall without ever seeing daylight. Happy days!' In Broadcasting House conditions varied. Many rooms had temporary air-conditioning, and the offices and studios could be noisy and uncomfortable. In the mid-1980s, in conversation with Colin Reid, Director-General Alistair Milne explained: 'Sadly Broadcasting House, so long the heart of the operation, has become obsolete. It is no longer a place in which to do modern radio … .We couldn't remain here much longer, patching up and replacing antiquated equipment … . Broadcasting House has kept wonderful traditions, but not even the Boardroom is big enough for all the board to assemble together.'

For Director-General John Birt, Broadcasting House was inefficient, expensive and archaic, and represented the 'worst aspects of the BBC'. Birt gave producers the power and control over their budgets to make their programmes elsewhere; Broadcasting House was not always the cheapest or most straightforward place to make a show. Simon Elmes, a BBC director at the time, later recalled: 'It was normal practice for the Studio Manager in B15 or 16 to say, "Can we just hold on – there's a Tube going past!" and wait till the rumble stopped! Then there was the old 8A drama studio near the canteen that was particularly prone to taxi radios which often broke through on to the programme circuits … .'

Fewer programmes were now being made in Val Myer's building, and it was straining under the weight of piecemeal changes made to it over the years. Studios were refurbished and suites of rooms occasionally converted. Meeting-rooms were created in the third-floor studio tower, a mezzanine level was inserted in the eighth-floor roof to provide extra office space, a new escalator improved the ground-floor connection to the extension and a new café was opened in 1995. The almost constant building work and the 'make do and mend' culture that persisted in the organization had left a building that was a long way beyond a patch-up job. Most staff had simply learned to live with the idiosyncrasies of Broadcasting House, and to work with what was available. There was a rumour circulating that any more holes made in the tower would cause it to collapse, and the ceilings were so crammed full of cables dating from the 1930s that it was nearly impossible to find room to put another wire. Even if one could find pockets of space in which to make improvements, there were scant records of what had previously been done to the building. Sorting this out would be problem enough in a house, but in a broadcasting building it was potentially disastrous.

In 1992, on the sixtieth birthday of Broadcasting House, the BBC offered public tours of the building. *The Independent* newspaper carried the headline, 'Once breathtaking, now comforting'. The tours were accompanied by an exhibition that allowed some of the corridors to be redecorated, but it was like papering over the cracks. The concert hall was refurbished in 1994, and its name was changed to the radio theatre. Although it was able to host concerts by the likes of David Bowie and REM, its public facilities were limited. Audiences had to queue outside, and there was nowhere to get a drink or leave a coat.

Three years later, and sixty-six years after retail space was first advertised, Broadcasting House finally got its shop on the ground floor of Portland Place. This led to the 'BBC Experience', an interactive exhibition and final attempt for Broadcasting House to become more audience-friendly. But despite its solid-looking appearance from the outside, the building was approaching the end of its working life. The final nail in its coffin came in 1998, when Radio News was moved (along with all non-World Service BBC journalists) to Television Centre at White City. The last *Today* programme was broadcast from studio 4A in Broadcasting House on 3 July 1998. Some journalists said that moving *Today* had finally torn the heart out of the building. Having survived the Second World War, the great battleship at the end of Regent Street had now become a ghost ship.

Opposite John Humphrys in the *Today* office on the day of the last edition made in Broadcasting House in 1998. Many journalists said that the decision to move the News department to new accommodation at White City finally tore the heart out of Broadcasting House.

Left Staff feeling about Broadcasting House was mixed, although for some (including the Director-General, John Birt) it represented an entrenched and old-fashioned culture, or 'the worst aspects of the BBC'. The 1990s were a particularly gloomy period for many working in Broadcasting House. Even in 2001, the dark corridors inside the building felt institutional and anonymous: not an appropriate image for the world's greatest broadcasting organization as it entered the twenty-first century.

2000

31 March The BBC's Director-General, Greg Dyke, launches 'One BBC' vision. Following this, the third floor of Broadcasting House is remodelled as open-plan space, and the BBC presents a preliminary feasibility study for Broadcasting House to its Governors.
September MacCormac Jamieson Prichard wins the commission to develop plans for a new extension to Broadcasting House.

2001

23 November Planning application is submitted for the redevelopment of Broadcasting House.

2002

27 June Planning consent is given by Westminster City Council for the redevelopment of Broadcasting House.
November Bovis Lend Lease is appointed to construct the redevelopment.
20 December Listed-building consent is granted for the internal remodelling of Broadcasting House.

2005

July Technical fit-out of the new building commences.
20 October MacCormac Jamieson Prichard's contract is terminated, and Sheppard Robson is appointed to take over the second phase of the redevelopment.

2006

January Completion of the first phase of the redevelopment. Broadcasting House and the new east wing are formally handed over to the BBC.
20 April The Queen reopens Broadcasting House and marks the eightieth anniversary of the granting of the Corporation's Royal Charter.
28 June Radio 3's *In Tune* is the first programme to be broadcast from the completed building.
20 November Demolition of the old extensions starts, in preparation for the next phase of building.

A Digital Voice

In recognition of its historic and cultural significance, and in an effort to protect it from losing its original character completely, Broadcasting House's Grade II listed-building classification was upgraded in 1995 to Grade II*, putting it in the top 8 per cent of the most important buildings in the country. At the same time something extraordinary was happening that would help to rescue what remained of Val Myer's building: the arrival of digital technology and the Internet. It was an expansive time for the BBC. Buoyed up by a new, technically charged confidence, it recruited staff to set up digital services and launched five new national radio stations. The organization wanted buildings to reflect the creative impetus, and now proposed grand building projects in Glasgow, Manchester and Birmingham. Listeners began to buy the smart new digital radios, and by 2001 nine out of ten adults were listening to the radio again.

In London it was decided to merge the separate BBC properties and bring London staff together on just three large sites: Broadcasting House, Television Centre and White City. White City was not a popular location among news journalists, and as the lease on the World Service's Bush House was ending, it was decided that BBC News, BBC Radio and Music and BBC World Service should be accommodated together in a new, larger building on the Broadcasting House site. In March 2000 the BBC's new Director-General, Greg Dyke, spoke about his vision for the future of the organization: 'Our aim is to create "One BBC", where people enjoy their job and are inspired and united behind the common purpose of making great programmes and delivering outstanding services.' Many of the staff listening to Dyke's message had been there during the loss of the Foster scheme, and were now in senior management themselves. Not only was this a chance to make amends architecturally but also, importantly, for an organization moving into the new millennium, a new building could provide the impetus to change working practices and create an iconic building for the new digital era.

The proposed 860,000-square-foot (80,000-sq.-m) Broadcasting House development would need to provide accommodation for 5000 staff and contain a huge newsroom, six television studios, and more than 140 acoustic studios and workshops. It was equivalent in size to about ten football pitches and would, in effect, transform Broadcasting House into one of the world's largest live-broadcast centres.

In the late summer of 2000 a competition was held to choose an architect to develop a vision for the project. The BBC

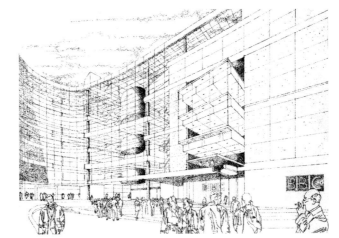

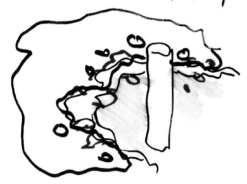

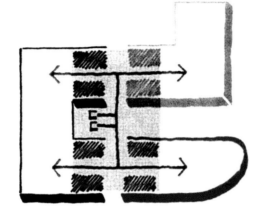

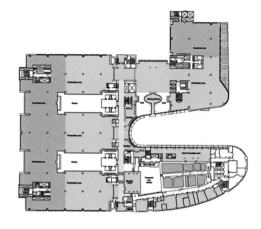

Above, left A sketch by Sir Richard MacCormac shows the concept of 'One BBC'. The idea of staff mixing echoed in some ways the informal atmosphere at Savoy Hill, so fondly recalled by early BBC staff. For MacCormac, the curving circulation space behind All Souls Church was analogous to a coastal shoreline, rich in ecology and a breeding ground for creativity.

Above, centre MacCormac's conceptual diagram translated on to the plan of the proposed new development, with Val Myer's building at the bottom right. Lifts and staircases were intended to serve a central thoroughfare and provide easy access to the production floors and the older building. The colours represent the notional zones of the three main directorates: News, Audio and Music and World Service.

Above, right A typical upper-floor plan of MacCormac Jamieson Prichard's design for the new development showing the disposition of studio spaces (purple) and production areas (green). The northern part of the extension (on the left) was designed specifically to take the heavier loads of the studios.

brought in respected advisers to put together a shortlist of six architectural practices. Stuart Lipton, then chairman of the Commission for Architecture and the Built Environment, was part of the selection process: 'Immediately we were treated as insiders and could demonstrate that best value was not necessarily the lowest cost. The most unusual part of the process was the full involvement of the chairman and most of the directors throughout. There was tangible excitement and enthusiasm and an understanding of the value of art to the value of the business.' Through its Director of Finance, Property and Business Affairs, John Smith, and the new architectural projects he was instigating, the BBC had rediscovered its interest in architectural patronage. Nearly seventy years after the completion of Broadcasting House, the organization looked set to find its architectural voice again. A new book, *Building the BBC: A Return to Form*, celebrated the BBC's resurgent interest in architecture and design, but with the sense of optimism and self-belief of the Corporation in the new century, its title might equally have been applied to the BBC as a whole.

The winning design

MacCormac Jamieson Prichard (MJP) was announced as the winner of the competition in November 2000. It joined other acclaimed practices Allies and Morrison and David Chipperfield Architects (who were working for the BBC at White City and in Glasgow respectively) in a new wave of design-focused architectural projects. Led by Sir Richard MacCormac, MJP had a long and respected track record in designing thoughtful and skilful buildings in historic settings. Its solution to the

Broadcasting House site was different from those of its competitors, who had all proposed new structures that deliberately contrasted architecturally with Val Myer's building. MJP wanted its new design to engage physically with Broadcasting House and embed itself into its surroundings. The practice's main idea was to create a backdrop of glass and stone behind the Grade I-listed All Souls Church. This would form the perimeter of a new public space between Val Myer's building and a new eastern extension to help draw people into the heart of the BBC. It was as though a protective arm had been put around Val Myer's building. The drum and spire of All Souls would be set against a subtly changing backdrop of layered glass, which would appear solid during the day. At night the situation would be reversed and the public would be able to peek through the veil of glass to see glimpses and shadows of the BBC at work.

The competition brief set by the BBC did not ask for detailed drawings, but for more creative sketches. MacCormac suggested that interstitial circulation spaces at the boundaries of departments might become fertile breeding grounds for ideas, and drew the analogy with a coastal shoreline, rich with diverse ecology. It is interesting to compare his sketch (above, left) with Reith's observation in 1932 that the BBC was less an organization, more a living organism (see page 43). MacCormac described Broadcasting House as a 'great convex, solid, rather masculine object which sits at the top of Regent Street in a very assertive way'. The new building would complement the solidity of Val Myer's building with a lightweight concavity and what MacCormac termed a 'supplicant convexity. … Just as in nature we understand

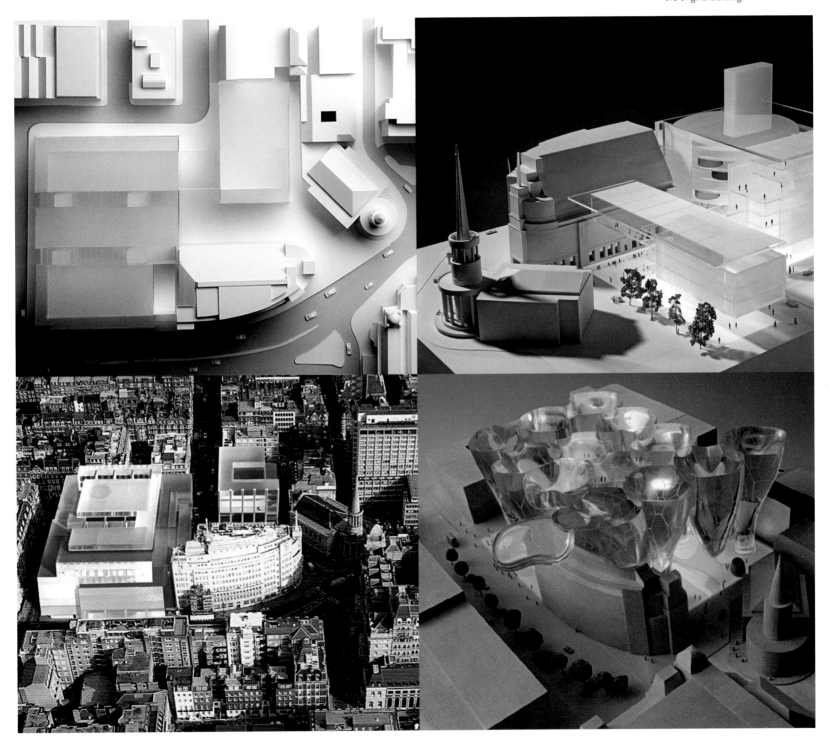

Models from the other entrants in the architectural competition run by the BBC in 2000 (clockwise from top left): Fletcher Priest; Stanton Williams; Alsop and Stormer; Eric Parry Architects. All these practices developed ideas for extensions in clear contrast with the original building.

a lot of natural experiences by the existence of opposites – such as night and day, heavy and light, male and female – following the logic of opposites enhancing each other, the new design explores the equivalent experiences in architecture: inside and outside, convexity and concavity, assertiveness and receptiveness, and opacity and transparency.'

The new building also defers to its urban setting by aligning on its main north–south axis with the spire of All Souls Church. The new east wing was set further back than the building it replaced, to create a new area of public realm on which a number of public facilities and the main staff entrance will be focused. It was originally envisaged that the existing one-way route for service traffic and taxis would need to be retained under the new building, but a successful planning application was subsequently made to remove the traffic completely.

MacCormac had identified the tribal nature and different cultures that had built up within the BBC over the years, and he was able to communicate this with characteristic charm and good humour. Jenny Abramsky, then Director of BBC Radio and Music, later recalled: 'I remember when I first met him, he just got what this building should be about. He had sympathy for it.' Perhaps even more crucially, he had realized that the method of what the BBC did in the building was invisible, and had decided to put the Corporation's thinking processes on show. MJP's new stone-and-glass façade attempted to convey the reassuring message that the new BBC could be both solid and transparent – a metaphor, if you like, for the Corporation as both reliable institution and accountable public service. The BBC's Alan Yentob called it 'a project of real conviction … a

respectful extension rather than a radical transformation'. Others described it simply as 'magical'.

The new extension was based on a straightforward E-shaped plan. The spine of the E, at the north end of the site, would support the heavier studios, with three wings of production offices reaching out to dramatic meeting spaces and circulation behind the new curved glass façade. The functions of this space meant that its light levels could be reduced. During the day much of the glass would appear opaque, but as twilight fell and the internal light level increased, the building could become transparent, until dawn, when the external light levels would dominate once more. The cyclical nature of the architecture would transform the building, in MacCormac's words, into 'a kind of theatre'. At the heart of the building would be an enormous open-plan newsroom, with four huge columns supporting the weight of the eight office floors above. MJP's project would allow people actually to see the news being made. On the ground floor a new 'street' would allow public access through the building to exhibitions, a café, a shop, the box office, reception and the bar for the radio theatre. Above this, double-height cafeterias, meeting spaces and thoroughfares interlocked on alternate floors via open staircases to give complex architectural form to Dyke's notion of 'One BBC'. These interconnecting spaces – MacCormac's 'shorelines' – were places where different teams and individuals could meet and exchange ideas.

Just as the BBC had set up a Studio Decoration Committee in 1932, a Design Steering Group was established to help develop and test ideas for the inside of the building. Its weekly

Opposite A study model exploring the relationship between internal and external lighting and the translucent façade envisaged in MJP's scheme. The façade would appear largely opaque during the day, to complement the solidity of Broadcasting House, and, as light levels changed, could become progressively more transparent, revealing the BBC at night while still having the potential to form a backdrop to the illuminated spire of All Souls Church.

Left An early model of the proposed scheme. Unlike the other competitors, MJP tried to join Val Myer's building seamlessly to the new extension. As in 1932, as much use had to be made of the site as possible. As well as having listed status, the site was in the Harley Street Conservation Area, near fourteen listed buildings, and in the protected view corridor from Primrose Hill to the Palace of Westminster. The proposed development was nine storeys high (135 feet/41 m) at its highest point, falling to eight and then six storeys on the eastern side of Langham Street, and stepping down to four storeys behind All Souls Church, with an area for satellite dishes set back at fifth-floor level. The new development would provide accommodation for around 2000 extra staff. To obtain planning consent for such a large building in a sensitive and complex area in a relatively short amount of time was perhaps an achievement equal to Val Myer's original project in 1932.

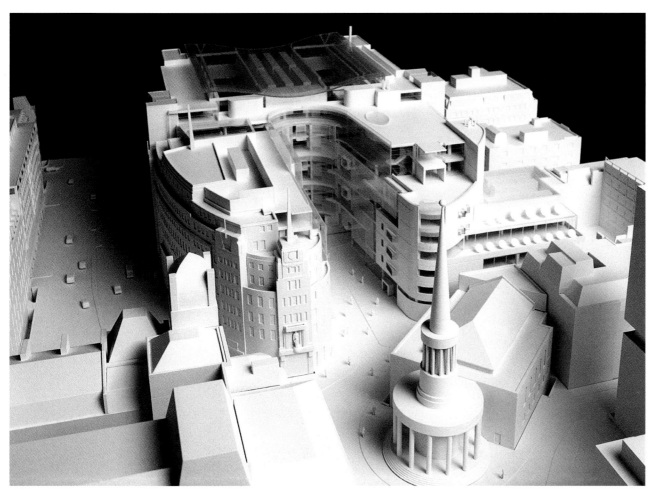

The new development would enable Broadcasting House to be fully refurbished, including major improvements to the radio theatre, in the heart of the building.

meetings were held at the BBC or at the architect's offices and continued, much less formally, in the local wine bar. The conversations helped to provide MJP with a valuable insight into the inner workings of the BBC, and allowed ideas from the competition stage of the project to be carried through into the new interior design of Broadcasting House. New open-plan production spaces in Val Myer's building would allow direct access to the studios, and a dramatic five-storey-high atrium was designed to expose the north wall of the studio tower and connect the various levels of the original building to the new extension. To achieve the ambitious original completion date of mid-2008, the design would need to be developed very quickly, and the ride through the process of gaining planning consent would need to be smooth. Despite MacCormac's reputation, the planners took some convincing that the project would fit into the surrounding area. In order to justify the idea of a large building, MJP encouraged others to think of the project in a wider historical context. As MacCormac explained:

I said, 'Here's the north-east corner of the Royal Opera House, which is adjacent to an 1820 town house half its height. Here is the British Museum, and here is a bit of Bloomsbury which it dominates', and everyone suddenly understood. In our case, here you have a national institution and alongside it the Georgian scale of Nash and Adam. This is the way it always was, until conservation officers started to believe that everything had to be the same scale.

This enabled MJP to resist the view of English Heritage (the government's adviser on historic buildings) that the new east wing of the extension behind All Souls Church should be smaller. This time, nobody suggested that the church be removed.

In October 2001, seven folders containing the planning application were submitted to Westminster City Council. At the planning committee meeting, Councillor Ian Wilder spoke of the 'incredible logistics of moving the world's greatest broadcasting operation, while having to maintain unbroken radio output', and on the warm summer evening of 27 June 2002, almost exactly seventy years after George V opened the original Broadcasting House, Westminster City Council unanimously granted planning consent for the project. The team was now faced with the prospect of delivering the new building over the next seven years. The impromptu celebrations that followed the committee's decision went on well into the evening and, for some of the exhausted team, the following day.

The gaining of planning approval set an enormous challenge as the project shifted immediately from design to delivery, and over the next few months there would be no let-up in the pace. It was a frenetic time: BBC Property staff, lawyers, bankers and numerous other consultants carried out the necessary financial checks and rapidly assembled the contracts and drawings that would make it possible to complete the financing of the project. The documentation would fill an entire room and describe in words and pictures the biggest transformation of Broadcasting House in its history. Work was divided into two phases: Broadcasting House and the new east wing of the extension would be constructed in the first phase, and the large new extension would be completed in the second.

Broadcasting House transformed

The wider ambitions behind the redevelopment provided a framework for thinking about how Broadcasting House could be used, and would allow the inside of Val Myer's building to be transformed. Staff were to move out for the duration of the refurbishment, allowing full access to Broadcasting House for the first time since its completion in 1932, and giving the opportunity to try to solve many of the long-term problems associated with broadcasting from the building. During the following six months the team made detailed plans to open up the dark corridors, silence the rumbling of trains in the basement, create new studios within the tower and new office spaces, preserve the best historic areas, squeeze in a completely new services infrastructure, and improve the building's environmental performance as much as possible. Perhaps just as importantly, the architects had to allay the fears of many BBC staff that the very special character and atmosphere of the building would be lost during the transformation.

The plan was to return a tower full of working broadcasting studios and programme-making production spaces to the original heart of Broadcasting House. It was an exciting prospect, but within a physically constrained, Grade II*-listed building it would not be easy. As part of the planning application, MJP had produced a study to define the historic significance of the individual spaces inside Broadcasting House. Now, an accurate measured survey and historic paint analysis were commissioned to discover more about the building. There was little existing information on what remained of the original design, and, even in the more intact rooms, it was hard to spot surviving architecture of 1932, as

much of the original interior had been replaced with lookalike fixtures and fittings. Fortunately, the original building had been well documented elsewhere, and good evidence of the original interiors, along with records of the many subsequent changes, had been kept in the London Metropolitan Archives. The few interiors that were original (or at least in the spirit of the original spaces) were defined as 'heritage areas', and it was decided that their historic features should be retained.

The other areas needed to be as flexible as possible. Broadcasting House was a building where electrical cables seemed to have a life of their own, occupying almost every cavity and constantly threatening to wriggle free. As the old wires were stripped out and the results of the measured surveys analysed it became clear that each floor had a different ceiling height, and that it would be immensely challenging to accommodate all the new services the BBC now demanded. But over the next few months, as the building gradually revealed itself, the team's knowledge accumulated. In August 2002 a listed-building application was made to remove the least historically significant internal walls, and three months later another was made, to replace the floors from the third floor of the studio tower upwards. This would provide greater acoustic protection for the new studios from the Underground running below.

In November 2002 Bovis Lend Lease was appointed to construct the building. Even for a contractor as experienced as Bovis, the project would prove to be an enormous challenge, not least because the BBC would need to continue to broadcast live from the old extension throughout the first

A series of studies in 1997 tested new methods of collaborative working. This resulted in the third floor of Broadcasting House being converted to open-plan use and helped to inform the designs for the new interior. This computer-generated image from 2003 shows a typical new open-plan production floor in Val Myer's Broadcasting House.

Below The floors in the studio tower were removed from the third level upwards in 2003 to help improve the acoustic performance of the studios in Broadcasting House. With access to the whole tower, the historic problem of noise from the Underground line could be finally solved.

Bottom Broadcasting House's vast roof was removed to allow the construction of four new floors.

Opposite Langham Street is seen during construction from the temporary bridge between the contractors' offices in Hallam Street and Broadcasting House. Under the builders' compound is a new basement linking Broadcasting House to the new east wing. In 2012 the area above it will become a public space.

In close-up (above) the extraordinary power and quality of Gill's sculpture are clear. *Prospero and Ariel* was carefully cleaned in the winter of 2004 with low-pressure water sprays and gentle brushing; during the process, Gill's secret sketch carving of a young girl (right) was found behind the statue.

phase of the project. Work began on site in December 2002, with the careful wrapping of Broadcasting House and the demolition of Egton House. In order to keep noise disruption to a minimum, special machines like roaming dinosaurs slowly took 'mouthfuls' of concrete from the east wing of the extension. Once the building had been eaten away, the construction of a huge three-storey-deep basement began alongside Broadcasting House, to provide the required 'resilience' for the development and to contain necessary plant, generators, space for deliveries, disabled car parking, service facilities and 300 bicycle spaces. The structural engineers monitored the surrounding buildings and the Underground line to detect any movement during the course of the project. The floor of the new basement would be just 13 feet (4 m) above the Victoria line tunnel, and to support the excavation and minimize vibration against existing buildings, sheet piles were driven in hydraulically to the edges of the site. As the excavation was completed during the following few months, more than 64,000 tons of debris were removed in 17,000 lorry-loads.

On the other side of the site, contractors struggled to keep the rain out of Broadcasting House while removing the vast roof and the upper floors of the studio tower. Four new floors of offices were then built above the fourth floor on the Langham Street side of the building. Inside Broadcasting House, all the heritage timber panelling was removed, cleaned and carefully reinstated, and Val Myer's concert hall and reception were refurbished. Above reception, all the existing office spaces were gutted and remodelled with completely new services. As the complexity and increased scope of the project placed pressure on the budget, the interior design had to be modified. The original plans for expensive hardwood finishes were dropped in favour of a series of more colourful and simply painted spaces. The coloured surfaces would echo the historic idea of Broadcasting House as a 'sound factory', and unify the interior. The painted surfaces would be easy to maintain and would allow the programme teams to create their own identities when they moved in. The painter Antoni Malinowski was selected by the BBC's new Public Art Group to provide colour advice for the interior and to develop a palette that complemented the original colours of the building. However, the designers did not have control over the whole interior, as the BBC decided to retain responsibility for the selection of the furniture, branding and special lighting within the building. This meant that the details, which had in 1932 so successfully

Left The radio theatre undergoing repair in the autumn of 2004. Various shades of stone-coloured paint were tried in the search for the best colour for television lighting.

Below During the repair of the council chamber each oak panel was numbered, removed from the site and carefully restored.

A typical production floor in the original Broadcasting House nears completion. The idea behind the new production spaces was to create an industrial-looking space or 'sound factory' for the twenty-first century. The long, narrow offices of the original building are now as open-plan as they can be, and the dark and confusing corridors have been opened up. A continuous recessed light against the studio tower illuminates the route around it, suggesting movement along the corridors and echoing the spirit of the original design. Dark-grey walls and a low ceiling reinforce the sense of being able to make a circuit of the exterior of the studios at the heart of the building, and disguise the technical risers along the route. Eventually the production spaces will open out into a dramatic light-filled atrium with bridge connections to the new building.

united the original interior and made the building memorable, would in 2006 lie outside the architect's control.

Part of the building was found to be suffering from 'Regent Street disease', a problem shared by many structures of a similar age in London's West End: water had slowly seeped through joints in the stonework and corroded the steel frame in the wall, cracking the stone. After repairs had been carefully completed, the windows were repainted and the Eric Gill sculptures and stone façade gently scrubbed with water.

Arts projects and the public art programme

The BBC was keen to extend its cultural remit by commissioning art for the new building, and several artists were selected by the Public Art Group and art consultant Modus Operandi to respond to the history and activity of Broadcasting House before it was closed for redevelopment.

One of the key images in George Orwell's novel *Nineteen Eighty-Four* was the infamous Room 101 at the Ministry of Truth. George Orwell worked at the BBC during the Second World War, and his time there partly inspired his bleak vision of the future. There was indeed a real Room 101, next to the general office on the eastern side of Broadcasting House. It was used for keeping staff records, but whether it had any connection with its fictional namesake is unclear. By 2003 it was a plant room. The idea of Room 101, however, remained so powerful that before the area was demolished to make way for the new extension, a cast was taken of the space by Rachel Whiteread and exhibited in the Cast Courts at the Victoria and Albert Museum until the end of June 2004 (above right).

Meanwhile, Tom Gidley filmed the empty corridors, offices and stairwells in Broadcasting House, Catherine Yass used a model helicopter to film the building from the air, and the drama studio and dramatic-effects store were recorded in *Presence*, a video made by Brian Catling. Nick Danziger and John Riddy were commissioned to document respectively the people and the architecture of the redevelopment, and Ron Haselden produced an interactive sculpture that offered the BBC's staff and visitors the opportunity to have their faces photographed on entry and then displayed on small screens around the building.

The BBC commissioned three permanent major artworks to enhance the completed redevelopment. MJP's competition idea to create a public space in Langham Street was complemented by Mark Pimlott's *World*, and in 2005 the BBC obtained planning consent from Westminster

City Council to close off the street completely. Pimlott's paving scheme (below right), which will be completed at the end of the project, has lines of latitude and longitude marked out in stainless steel and brass; engraved into the granite will be 750 place-names significant to the BBC, from Ambridge to Baghdad. As part of the artwork, a network of floor-mounted speakers will broadcast the languages of the World Service.

The light sculpture *Breathing*, a collaboration between Jaume Plensa and Sir Richard MacCormac, was installed on the roof of the east wing of the new development in 2005, and was subsequently dedicated as a memorial to all news journalists and their crews killed in action. The inverted glass cone, based on the spire of All Souls Church, projects a vertical beam of light about 3000 feet (900 m) into the night sky. Special consent had to be obtained from the Civil Aviation Authority, as the sculpture lies under the flight path to London City Airport. Another poem, *Memorial*, was commissioned from James Fenton and will appear in the second phase of the building when it is complete:

We spoke, we chose to speak of war and strife –
a task a fine ambition sought –
and some might say, who shared our work, our life:
that praise was dearly bought.

Artists Martin Richman and Tony Cooper designed a lighting scheme to link Broadcasting House and All Souls Church, and to highlight both buildings at night.

As well as the permanent artworks, a series of images was commissioned for temporary site hoardings on the prow of Broadcasting House during construction (overleaf). Fiona Rae produced *Signal*, a computer-generated collage, and *Acts of Inscribing* by William Furlong was a photograph and recording of the Broadcasting House sound-effects store (the guests staying at the Langham Hotel were bemused by some of the strange noises it incorporated). The winning entry to a *Blue Peter* competition showed a cutaway drawing of Broadcasting House, and the graffiti-like *On Air* was created by children from All Souls Primary School, the school closest to Broadcasting House. Liz Rideal's *Kerfuffle* was the final and perhaps the most popular image, and celebrated the BBC's role as a showbiz producer. It showed pairs of hands poised to draw back red curtains to reveal the newly refurbished building.

Opposite The completed external lighting scheme by Martin Richman and Tony Cooper links Broadcasting House and All Souls Church.

Above Rachel Whiteread's plaster cast of Room 101, *Untitled (Room 101)* (top) and Mark Pimlott's *World*, a proposal for the new pedestrian space in Langham Street.

During its repair, Broadcasting
House was covered in a series of
artist-designed hoardings: *Kerfuffle* by
Liz Rideal (opposite); *Signal* by Fiona
Rae (above, left); and *Acts of Inscribing*
by William Furlong (above, centre
left). The winning design (above,
centre right) from the *Blue Peter*
competition, by Leo Thomson (aged
nine), featured a cross-section of
Broadcasting House with different
programmes being made in each
room (including the Queen reading
her Christmas message, and even a
member of BBC staff enjoying a bath);
and *On Air* (above, right) was made
by pupils of All Souls Primary School,
curated by Cloth of Gold artists.

Broadcasting House reopens

Fantastic! You haven't ruined a building I've known for years.
BBC staff member, on being shown round the newly
refurbished building

In January 2006, after three years of building work, involving
the creation of nearly 180,000 square feet (16,600 sq. m) of
new and refurbished floor space, twenty-seven new acoustic
areas and studios within the tower, more than 10,000 drawings
and more than forty separate listed-building submissions,
Broadcasting House was ready to be handed back to the BBC.
This significant moment was overshadowed somewhat by
disagreements between MacCormac and the construction
management team over the detailed design of the second
phase. The BBC, Bovis and Land Securities had issued a
joint statement on 24 October 2005, declaring that they
had decided that MJP would not be continuing with the
redevelopment, because of 'creative differences' between the
parties. Architectural practice Sheppard Robson was engaged
to take on the second part of the project, with a revised
completion date of 2012.

As the remaining architectural and technical work was
completed, BBC staff were gradually moved back into
Broadcasting House, and by September 2006 it was once
again fully occupied. Inside there was space for about
500 people, with nearly 400 desks for making radio
programmes. The various teams moving into the new
open-plan offices included staff working for Radio 3,
Radio 4, Audio and Music, Factual, the Children's Unit,
Consumer Programmes, BBC7 and Information & Archives.
Fire and security teams and various catering staff also moved
back into the building. A temporary ground-floor café
provided them all with an important social hub.

Broadcasting House was certainly lighter and brighter,
and – perhaps most importantly – quieter. In addition, the
refurbished building was given an official 'Excellent' rating
for energy-efficiency. Broadcasting House was working better
than ever before.

Her Majesty The Queen visited on Thursday 20 April 2006,
an occasion that formed part of her own eightieth birthday
celebrations and also marked the eightieth anniversary of the
granting of the Corporation's Royal Charter. To symbolize the
start of a new era for Broadcasting House, the Queen unveiled
a plaque commemorating the reopening of the building, and
was given a digital radio as a present.

On Wednesday 28 June 2006, after more than three years
of silence, Val Myer's building was finally switched back on
to begin once more broadcasting live to the world. Just as in
1932, the first programme came from the large studio at the
top of the building. Even discerning listeners to Radio 3's
In Tune would not notice any difference, but for everyone
starting to work in Broadcasting House, the building had
been transformed. Its symbolic power and distinctive
atmosphere had been preserved, perhaps even enhanced,
for those visiting or broadcasting from it. The refurbished
building would take the democratic monumentality of
Val Myer's architecture into the twenty-first century, and
bring digital broadcasting with it. Comparing Broadcasting
House with the new British Library in Roger Stonehouse
and Gerhard Stromberg's *The Architecture of the British Library at
St Pancras* (2004), MacCormac suggested that both buildings
could now be said to create direct relationships with the
individuals who would use and visit them: 'The singularity
of its architecture enables it to symbolize its widely shared
cultural purpose. This kind of monumentality is not imposed
upon us; it is assigned by us. ... You are [now] invited to be a
participant, not merely a spectator.' The future of Broadcasting
House as a place to lift the spirit had been secured.

A Tour of Broadcasting House in 2007

BH is solid, confident, obtuse.
Jenny Abramsky, Director of Audio and Music, June 2007

Broadcasting House and radio belong together: the building is a lens through which we can follow the fortunes of British radio. It was a building destined for change even before it was finished in 1932: specialization, technological improvement and continued expansion were inevitable. For all its idiosyncrasies, Val Myer's building proved remarkably robust. It provided a framework within which a creative organization could experiment; it offered the chance to make mistakes; and it conveyed a powerful message to its occupants. Some rooms remained reassuringly unchanged for decades, yet some (less public) spaces were altered beyond recognition. Importantly, enough survives to act as a reminder of the building's original aspirations and ideals.

In a wider context, Broadcasting House offers an example of how a historic building can be reused and revitalized with vision, determination, conviction and imagination. Of course, it is fortunate that the original tenant is still in residence, but if a building as technically complex and spatially constrained as this can be saved, almost any other surely can. The new infrastructure that has been so carefully woven into the refurbished Broadcasting House was installed with change in mind, and should allow the healthy tension between the building and its occupier to continue.

We begin the tour, as we did in the 1930s, at the top of the building. The programmes that are now made here can be heard on Radio 3, Radio 4 and BBC7. On the third floor is a new control room (forty years after the last one was removed), in the basement the music library has returned, and the refurbished radio theatre is busier than it has ever been. The building is fully digital and ready to face new challenges. For all the changes it has undergone over the years, Broadcasting House remains a 'factory of sound'.

The carefully cleaned Broadcasting House stands alone at the end of the first phase of the development. Val Myer's ivory tower is at last being opened up to allow more people to see inside. The discreet new extension is barely visible at the top of the building.

Eighth floor

Studio 80A One of the largest studios in the building, this is the only one to be naturally lit. The original porthole windows from the Chermayeff studio have been unblocked and reused. Two cubicles face each other across the double-height space, with the timber floor providing a lively acoustic. The studio is large enough for recitals and is used for many different programmes, including the daily Radio 3 *In Tune* programme and Radio 4's *Loose Ends*. Guests have already included Sting, Curtis Stigers, James Galway and the Ukelele Orchestra of Great Britain (above). The design echoes that of the original studio (see page 57), with its reflective horizontal banding.

Seventh floor

Seventh-floor library A new double-height space for a library and meeting-room was created at the top of the building by removing the old eighth-floor waiting-room. The light-filled space has a view on to the new terrace and is overlooked by the new green room for studio 80A.

60A: Drama studio This new double-height studio was designed for drama production and can be used to create many different sound effects. It is rather like an acoustic playground, and is the modern equivalent of the Wells Coates studio on page 65.

The room is unusual because it contains two full flights of stairs. This distance in the space is important, as it means that actors do not need to improvise with their voice or footsteps. The staircases have treads that are covered half in timber and half in stone to create

different effects (above, bottom right). The room upstairs can be used for bedroom scenes (above, centre right). This is necessary because voices sound different when people are lying down. The 'snail', in the corner of the studio (above, top right), is a small, spiralling corridor that is heavily acoustically insulated and exaggerates acoustic perspective, an effect that Val Gielgud wanted to achieve in the 1930s. When a performer walks into the snail, his or her voice rapidly grows quieter, creating the illusion of distance in a confined space. Despite being in the heart of London's West End,

the space inside the snail can be used for any number of scenes, including those set in the countryside at night.

Different materials on the floors and walls create different acoustics. A curtain or screen can be pulled across the studio to create two smaller spaces with two types of acoustic, and a carpet can be rolled out for different floor effects. Various doors, knockers, latches, chains and windows create different sounds, and there is even a working kitchen sink, since discerning listeners can detect the difference in sound between hot and cold water.

New production offices

The production spaces are for the production teams that make both live and pre-recorded radio programmes. Live programmes made in Broadcasting House today include *Woman's Hour*, *You and Yours* (fifth floor), *Start the Week*, *Midweek*, *Excess Baggage*, *Thinking Allowed*, *In Our Time* (sixth floor) and the pre-recorded programmes *Desert Island Discs* and *The Food Programme*.

The *Woman's Hour* office (above) on the new fifth floor is typical of the open-plan spaces that were created following the removal of Val Myer's

roof, with a lighter, brighter working environment than the older spaces below. After years of staff cutting tape with razor blades, Broadcasting House is officially tape-less, and for the first time the production process is digital from beginning to end. Broadcasting House is quieter these days because of its improved acoustic performance, but also because production spaces are open-plan, which means that staff wear headphones to edit material. Programmes are assembled and edited in adjacent, acoustically separate spaces called workshops and woffices, which are part workshop, part office.

Keeping the building quietly cool was one of the biggest challenges. However, through the carefully integrated design of the lighting, electrical, technical, cooling and ventilation services, the opening up of production spaces on every floor means that the majority of the working spaces in Broadcasting House feel calmer, more generous and more comfortable than ever before. New secondary glazing in every original window means that the problem of traffic noise from Portland Place has also finally been solved.

A *Woman's Hour* team meeting is chaired by presenter Jenni Murray in one of the new glazed meeting-rooms in the prow of the building.

The newspapers are studied each day for topical features, and whiteboards display the names of guests for both recording and transmission. Noticeboards are littered with the usual office paraphernalia as well as audience ratings, programme reviews and listener correspondence.

A newspaper article published in the early 1930s reported that the decision to ventilate the studios artificially, and the consequent extra ductwork in the ceilings, might have meant that Lord Reith would have trouble standing up in his new building (he was 6 feet 6 inches/ 2 m tall). In 2001 the problem of squeezing the vast number of new services into the corridors around the studio tower while retaining a reasonable ceiling height was once again a major concern for the BBC. Most of the technical wires and cables in the building are hidden from view in riser cupboards that surround the studio tower. The grooves in the cupboard walls have been designed to match the dimensions of standard BBC signage.

Woffices The woffices function as a cross between a workshop and an office. They allow producers and presenters to listen to programmes on loudspeakers without disturbing colleagues in open-plan spaces. The simple repeating pattern on the walls of the woffices helps to provide acoustic absorption and softly reflects the light. It also echoes Val Myer's decorative wave theme around the building.

Staircases The original staircases contribute greatly to the unique atmosphere of Broadcasting House. The original character has been retained while the legibility of the circulation around the building is increased. The worn steps have been left as a memory of the thousands of staff who have run between floors, and the artificially lit windows have been repaired. Vibrant colours create an internal narrative that helps to orientate the visitor and complements the more subdued original colours. The outside of the repaired tower is painted in vermilion, which highlights its importance (see pages 136–37),

and inside the colour changes to light battleship grey, to represent the 'engine room' of the building. The south-west staircase leads from the temple-like reception area to the hallowed hall of the council chamber, and is painted the original white (above, bottom left). The others have been painted light battleship grey or a shade of ochre – light buff, mid-buff or deep buff – to match the design of 1932.

A typical studio Traditionally, programmes needed a producer, a studio manager and a presenter. In the *Woman's Hour* studio (above), the presenter and contributors sit at a fabric-covered table (to prevent noise), and the producer and studio manager sit in the adjacent cubicle. The studio manager looks after the technical quality of the programme while the producer takes editorial control of the content.

Today, the traditional roles of producer, studio manager and presenter are less defined, and the studios in Broadcasting House can in theory be used for any station, providing they contain the right equipment.

The painterly approach to the new interior continues in the finishes of the new studios. Painted perforated-timber panels are designed to be removable, to allow studios to be 'tuned' to different degrees of reverberation. The horizontal banding between the joints in the timber panels echoes the 1930s studios.

Announcer Ian Skelly at work in the Radio 3 continuity studio (top). Guests appearing on *Desert Island Discs* since the reopening of Broadcasting House have included Ricky Gervais, George Michael, Oliver Postgate and, of course, Bagpuss (above), pictured with presenter Kirsty Young.

Continuity studios The art of radio continuity has become more technically sophisticated over the years, and a relatively recent development is the 'self-operation studio'. This makes use of modern digital technology to obviate the need for a separate studio manager or producer. The sound levels and balance are controlled by the announcer or presenter, who is also solely responsible for keeping the network on air. The continuity studio controls the output of the network and fills in any gaps between programmes. Radio 4 continuity is run this way, with the continuity announcer in studio 40B

being the last pair of ears in the chain before the signal goes to the transmitters. With programmes of different lengths, trails to play and the shipping forecast to read, there is a lot to think about, and the continuity announcer's calm voice belies the complexity of the task.

The best continuity announcers possess an unassuming presence. Peter Jefferson (above) joined the BBC in 1964, and now works as a freelance announcer on Radio 4. As one listener put it, his voice has 'decorum and authority, laced with a warming trace of friendliness'.

Overleaf The *Woman's Hour* studio is seen from the seats of the producer and studio manager at the cubicle control desk.

The council chamber The historic panelling of the council chamber was carefully dismantled and a later finish painstakingly removed before it was restored to its original appearance by means of French polishing. A new timber floor had to be laid, as asbestos was discovered underneath the old one. Above the fireplace hangs a portrait of Sir John Reith by the painter Oswald Birley (1880–1952). The work captures Reith's intense gaze, which, according to an early BBC employee, could make one feel like 'a couple of threepenny bits'.

Today the room is used for presentations, meetings (also by the BBC Trust), events and the occasional party.

The BBC coat of arms Adopted by the Corporation in March 1927 to represent its purpose and values, the coat of arms has changed considerably over time. This representation was placed opposite the fireplace, above the original chairman's seat, and was by George Kruger Gray (1880–1943), an English artist best known for his coins and stained glass. The lion shows that the BBC is British; in a representation of broadcasting, it grasps a thunderbolt in its paw. The eagles symbolize the speed of broadcasting, and suspended from their collars are bugles, which stand for 'proclamation' or the public-

service element of the BBC. The globe represents the breadth of the BBC's operations. Around it are seven estoiles, heraldic symbols symbolizing divine goodness and nobility, reinforcing the scope of the Corporation. They also represent the seven planets known at the time of the BBC's founding. The background of the shield, the mantling (drapery) on the helmet above the shield, and the collars of the eagles are blue – or azure, to use the accurate heraldic term.

The BBC motto, 'Nation shall speak peace unto Nation', was probably inspired by a biblical verse from the books of Micah (4:3) and

Isaiah (2:4): 'Nation shall not lift up sword against nation, neither shall they learn war any more.' The motto was changed in 1934 to '*Quaecunque*', meaning 'Whatsoever', taken from the dedication '*Deo Omnipotenti*' in reception and inspired by the letter of St Paul to the church in Philippi (Philippians 4:8): 'Finally, brethren, whatsoever things are true, … whatsoever things are just, whatsoever things are pure, whatsoever things are of good report; if there be any virtue, and if there be any praise, think on these things.'

The London control room

A room that is hidden away but carries out much of the vital work of Broadcasting House is the London control room, the technical hub for the BBC's national radio services. Programme audio from Broadcasting House studios, studios at other BBC sites and computer replay systems passes through equipment in the basement apparatus room of Broadcasting House. This complex equipment is maintained and controlled by London control-room staff, using an array of touch-controlled computer screens. These systems ensure that the correct programme source is routed to the correct destination; for example, that the studio currently occupied by Radio 3 is feeding Radio 3's FM, DAB, Freeview, Satellite and Internet transmission platforms. London control-room staff can listen to many different points in the broadcast chain to find a problem if one does occur, and can change over to resilient equipment in another location to ensure that output is maintained at full quality. This is usually achieved without having any impact on the audience.

The London control room is also the centre for receiving lines from outside broadcasts, such as *Any Questions* and *Friday Night is Music Night*. The staff test each circuit to make sure that it is of the correct quality for the broadcast before connecting it to the relevant transmission studio.

Lifts Hopton-Wood stone is a light-coffee-coloured limestone from Derbyshire, with a cool, marble-like quality. The fossil shells embedded in it have been highly polished in the entrance hall of Broadcasting House to reveal their full beauty. The subtlety of Val Myer's work with the material can also be seen in the scalloped, wave-patterned carving that provides subtle relief and soft shadows over the lift doors.

The actor Maurice Denham was apprenticed as a young man to Waygood-Otis and helped to maintain the lifts at Broadcasting House. He recalled:

I was responsible for servicing those lifts. I had to straddle the girders on top of them to be winched gradually up to the eighth floor. I had large tins of grease, which I poured into the cups and poles either side of the elevators as we slowly descended down the eleven floors. There were no indicators in those lifts. The floor numbers were housed in a little toy cage, attached to a piece of catgut. The catgut stretched badly, so I had to tie knots in it.

The lifts have been restored to their former appearance, and retain the bronze-painted doors and BBC logo in the floor and lift call panel. White glass panels have been added to the walls to match the Art Deco light fittings and artists' lobby. The Art Deco lights have been remade and the lift lobby repainted light battleship grey to represent its function as the main circulation space inside the studio tower. The idea of opposites in the architecture of the building is continued internally, as the colour could also be seen as the inverse of the vermilion red used on the outside of the tower.

Ground floor

Reception Broadcasting House is more secure today than it has ever been. Previously, security guards and a rope were all that prevented people from gaining access to the building. Now, a carefully designed glass screen provides improved security inside the building. A new white-glass reception desk echoes the high-level Art Deco lighting. Since the new building was opened the BBC has installed leather seating against the wall and an interactive display.

On the left wall of the entrance lobby is a stone commemorating the original building team. On the right wall, another plaque reads: 'Their Majesties King George and Queen Mary honoured the building with their presence on July 7th 1932'. Underneath is the plaque installed when the Queen reopened Broadcasting House on 20 April 2006. On the east wall of reception itself is a roll of honour, remembering members of BBC staff who lost their lives in the Second World War.

The new position of the reception desk emphasizes the symmetry of the space and draws attention to the famous inscription above, the BBC logo in the floor and Gill's sculpture *The Sower*. Before radio gave the word another meaning, 'to broadcast' referred to the scattering of seeds. The sculpture is a metaphor of one of the biblical parables, a story Jesus told in which seed that fell on fertile ground yielded a good harvest. Gill wrote to his brother Cecil: 'Comic thought, when you consider the quality of BBC semination, to compare it with the efforts of a simple countryman sowing corn.'

Artists' lobby The artists' lobby, which leads to the studio tower, is one of the more intact original spaces in Broadcasting House. Its sparse character has been reinforced by light-battleship-grey walls and a simple white-glass screen. This provides extra illumination in the windowless space and makes a visual connection with reception and the new lift interiors. The BBC has also coloured the light and added network branding.

In place of the former information boards is a tapestry dating from April 1949 (above). It was presented to the BBC on behalf of the French people in recognition of the help and comfort offered by London Radio in the dark days of the German occupation. Called *The Poet*, it was specially designed by Jean Lurçat and is based on a poem entitled 'Liberté' by Paul Eluard. The tapestry depicts a member of the Maquis (the secret army of patriots in France during the occupation) hidden in a leafy grotto receiving messages from a carrier pigeon and a fish, 'symbolic of the information received from the air from the BBC'.

Radio theatre While the second phase is being completed, this space remains one of London's more secret venues. The original public entrance lobby on Portland Place was always too small, and Val Myer's planned extension showed the intention to provide a larger foyer. Seventy-five years later, the audience is still patiently queuing outside to get in, but in 2012 the theatre will finally have more facilities and a clearer presence on the street.

A series of performances marked the reopening of the radio theatre in 2007. Enter Shikari played (top) and Stephen Fry and Matt Lucas took part in BBC Network Radio's fortieth anniversary celebrations (above). The refurbishment has brought renewed vitality to Broadcasting House, and will help to make the radio theatre a more attractive venue than ever before. Acts that have performed in this intimate hall since its reopening include Radiohead, Jack Johnson and Katie Melua.

The radio theatre has been given a new floor at a higher level, allowing easier access from the street for both audience and performers. Stage lifts provide access to a large storage area underneath the floor, and a new, oak-clad cubicle below the upper gallery level incorporates an eighty-track recording facility and mixing desk. The walls of the theatre have been repainted in a warm stone colour to complement the original architecture, and new lighting has been carefully positioned to highlight the original pilasters and architectural decoration. The Art Deco light fittings have also been repaired and fitted with coloured lights. The 312 seats can be removed to accommodate a larger, standing audience. Technical rigging, stage lighting, special-effect lighting, video and computer projection, conference PA sound, press and live broadcast sound, video cameras, audio and video recording, and satellite links have been installed to allow the theatre to be used for television broadcasts.

As well as being used by the BBC, the radio theatre is now a versatile venue for live events, product launches, conferences, awards ceremonies, and film and photographic shoots.

New uplighters were carefully
positioned to highlight the coffered
pilasters and complement the Art
Deco lighting. The microphones
suspended above the seating are
for the audience.

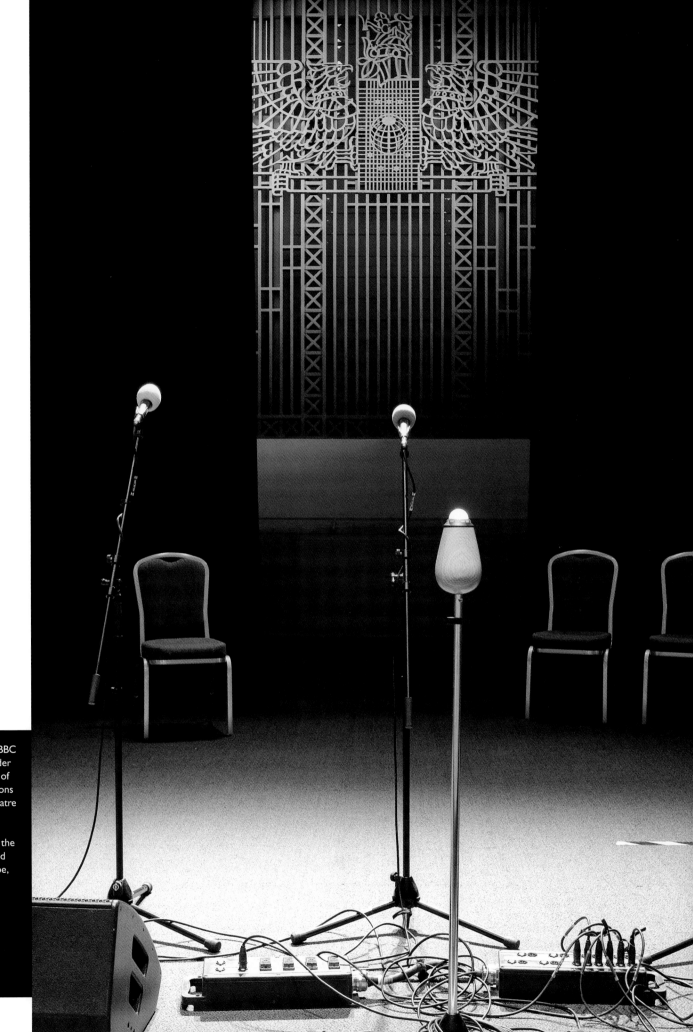

The bronze organ grille with the BBC crest (right) is a constant reminder to performers and the audience of the role and the original aspirations of the BBC. At the back of the theatre (overleaf) is a new, fully glazed viewing room for meetings and private events. External users of the radio theatre have so far included *The Observer*, *The Guardian*, Adobe, British Airways, Energis, Ernst & Young and the British Council.

Radio theatre dressing-rooms
The three dressing-rooms for performers are next to the radio theatre on the lower ground floor. The previous changing-rooms for performers were extremely limited. The new rooms are decorated with landscape-themed wallpaper, inspired by murals in the original basement listening-rooms.

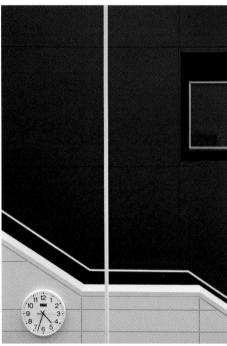

Information & Archives The
new double-height space for the
Information & Archives department
is in the old vaudeville studio in the
basement of the building, and is a
music-lover's dream. This is where
many of the BBC's music CDs are
kept. The archive contains 310,000
individual CDs, 20,000 boxed sets
and 20,000 recordings, from fragile
reel-to-reel recordings to the
Radio 1 archive, including the now-
famous John Peel sessions. An annual
budget of £77,000 allows the team
to buy 200–300 new CDs every
week (mainly from HMV). Ten vans
make daily deliveries of CDs to the
other BBC radio stations across
the UK. Orders placed before
3.30 pm are guaranteed to arrive
the following day in the four major
BBC centres (Bristol, Birmingham,
Manchester and Cardiff), and the
same guarantee is made for other
London sites if an order is made
before 5.30 pm. Vinyl recordings are
stored offsite, at the BBC's premises
in Windmill Road, west London.
   Despite being three storeys
below ground, the archive is bright
and spacious. To make the team feel
part of the world above, the same
materials and colours were used as
in the studios.

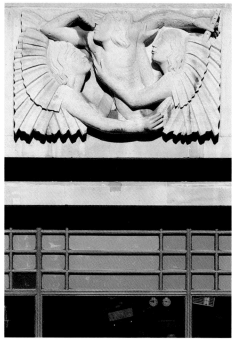
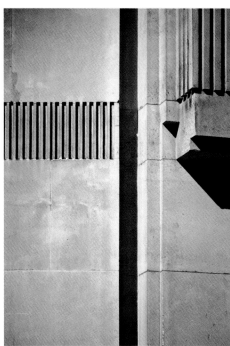

Decoration A repeating wave pattern appears above the entrance doors (top left), and can also be found at cornice level in the lifts. The incised decoration of Val Myer's building is classically inspired (bottom left). This is a building that can hold a shadow only for a fleeting moment.

Gill's *Ariel Hearing Celestial Music* above the large shop window on Portland Place (top right) is not taken from *The Tempest*; it may have come instead from inside the BBC. The simple, almost childlike low-relief sculptures on the exterior

of the building are strongly narrative. The delicate Georgian-style windows that Val Myer loved have been refurbished (bottom right). Paint analysis revealed that they were originally a light battleship grey, which would have visually recessed them and emphasized the contrast with the Portland stone walls.

The keystone one might expect to find over the entrance is substituted with a globe on which stands a large sculpture of Prospero and Ariel (opposite). Gill stated in *The Listener* on 15 March 1933 that he was not generally in favour of sculptures on buildings, because he thought the sculptor 'was only called in to titivate a building which it [was] supposed would otherwise be too dull and plain'. *Prospero and Ariel* was an exception, however, because it had its own niche: 'The sculpture proclaims who the building belongs to and what game they think they are playing at. The Governors of the BBC are obviously playing a very

high game indeed. *Deo Omnipotenti* are the first words they hurl at you in their entrance hall, and so the choice of what should be placed in the niche over the main door was obviously a difficult matter.'

The actor Leslie French, who was playing the part at the time at Sadler's Wells, was Gill's model for Ariel. The religious theme is conveyed by the raising of Ariel's arms (as if in Christ's act of supplication), and his hands bear stigmata. However, Fiona MacCarthy suggests in her biography of Gill (1989) that the true inspiration for Ariel was not French, nor God the Father and Son, but Gill's own

adopted son, Gordian: 'It's a larger-scale version of the *Foster Father* [an earlier Gill sculpture]: the father hieratic, wise, protective, optimistic, closer to a Gill self-portrait than the Prospero of Shakespeare; the son nervy, tense and eager but bound closely to his father. This was Gill's hopeful, vulnerable version of Gordian.'

THE BRITISH
BROADCASTING CORPORATION

Extension and new wing As well as the conservation and repair of Broadcasting House, the basement and exterior of a new east wing were also completed. Its design echoes the prow of Broadcasting House (above, right). The light sculpture by Jaume Plensa and Richard MacCormac on the roof of the new wing continues the BBC's commitment to public art in the twenty-first century, and matches the spire of All Souls Church and the mast on top of Broadcasting House.

The new double-skinned façade at the top of Broadcasting House replaces Val Myer's slate roof. The new extension does not touch the original stone, and the glass is separated from the older building by a groove running around the new façade. The inner glazing forms the building's weathertight envelope, and the outer layer acts as a solar shield. It is decorated with a ceramic fritted pattern and tones with the Portland stone below.

The upper-level extension allows previously unseen views from the top half of the building. An internal balcony between the two layers of glazing on the sixth floor provides a view down Regent Street.

The completion of Broadcasting House's refurbishment signalled the start of the fitting out of the east wing. This building will eventually be home to a number of departments, including the new BBC Arabic television service. Broadcasting House is complemented by the architectural treatment of the new wing. The new stone was chosen to match the original façade, and a glass slot expresses the connection between old and new. The thin edge of the glazing is visible and reflects the sky. Lines were incised in the stone to echo the stripped classical decoration of the original building.

The completed first phase is seen from a first-floor bedroom in the Langham Hotel in the summer of 2007. The desire to reflect the architecture of Val Myer's Broadcasting House can be clearly seen. The second phase of construction, taking place behind the blue hoardings, will unite the two buildings above ground and create a new public space. It is scheduled for completion in 2012.

Sources

Archives

BBC written archives at Caversham, Berkshire

BBC photographic archives at White City, west London

London Metropolitan Archives

Royal Institute of British Architects Library and Photograph Collection

Publications

Architectural Review vol. 2, no. 429, August 1932

Simon Bradley and Nikolaus Pevsner, *The Buildings of England*, London 6: Westminster, London (Yale University Press) 2003

Asa Briggs, *The Golden Age of Wireless* (vol. 2 of The History of Broadcasting in the United Kingdom), London (Oxford University Press) 1965

British Broadcasting Corporation, *Broadcasting House*, London (BBC) 1932

British Broadcasting Corporation, *A Technical Description of Broadcasting House*, London (BBC) 1932

John Cain, *The BBC: 70 Years of Broadcasting*, London (BBC) 1992

Wilfrid Goatman, *By-ways of the BBC*, London (P.S. King & Son) 1938

Freddie Grisewood, *My Story of the BBC*, London (Odhams Press) 1959

David Hendy, *Life on Air: A History of Radio Four*, Oxford (Oxford University Press) 2007

Tom Hickman, *What Did You Do in the War, Auntie? The BBC at War 1939–45*, London (BBC) 1995

Nicola Jackson, *Building the BBC: A Return to Form*, London (Wordsearch/BBC) 2003

R.S. Lambert, *Ariel and All His Quality: An Impression of the BBC From Within*, London (Gollancz) 1940

Fiona MacCarthy, *Eric Gill*, London (Faber and Faber) 1989

MacCormac Jamieson Prichard, *BBC Broadcasting House Development*, Heritage Study Part Two, 2001

New Architecture: Foster, Rogers, Stirling, exhibition catalogue by Deyan Sudjic, London, Royal Academy of Arts, 3 October– 21 December 1986

Alan Powers, *Britain: Modern Architectures in History*, London (Reaktion Books) 2007

— *Serge Chermayeff: Designer, Architect, Teacher*, London (RIBA Publishing) 2001

Steen Eiler Rasmussen, *London: The Unique City*, London (Jonathan Cape) 1937

Colin Reid, *Action Stations: A History of Broadcasting House*, London (Robson Books) 1987

Guy Saich, 'History of BBC Broadcasting House', unpublished research and part of planning submission, 2001

Robert Wood, *A World in Your Ear: The Broadcasting of an Era, 1923–1964*, London (Macmillan) 1979

Various BBC yearbooks and handbooks

Websites

arthurlloyd.co.uk

bbc.co.uk

Roger Beckwith, 'Old Radio Broadcasting Equipment and Memories', orbem.co.uk

Mike Todd, 'Broadcasting House: A Potted History', miketodd.net/ other/bhhistory

Acknowledgements

Broadcasting, architecture and publishing are both creative and technical disciplines, needing a wide range of skills and teams of people. The vast number of people who were involved in the refurbishment of Broadcasting House, and who have given their time to this book during the last seven years, would fill an entire chapter.

However, I am particularly grateful to a number of individuals and organizations. The sponsors have provided the generous support necessary to make the book viable, and include many of the people who rebuilt Broadcasting House from the inside out. I was especially fortunate to work closely with many dedicated colleagues and friends at MacCormac Jamieson Prichard Architects, especially Chris Burrows, King Chong, Jeremy Estop, Michael Evans, Andrew Frood, Peter Jamieson, Andy Jones, Lucy Jones, Simon Kennedy, Peter Kent, Sir Richard MacCormac, Duncan McKinnon, Richard Moorby, Richard Robinson, David Rose and Daniel Shabetai. I hope this book goes a little way towards illustrating your achievement. To all the many hundreds of other people involved in the redevelopment of Broadcasting House, Reith's words to his staff on opening the building in 1932 seem appropriate: 'I look forward, and nothing but forward'!

The close cooperation of the BBC has been essential in making the researching and writing of this book so enjoyable. Many BBC staff (old and new) have put up with my constant intrusions into their home for nearly seven years, including those in Audio and Music, Information & Archives, and several key individuals: Jenny Abramsky,

David Anderson, Keith Beale, Tim Cowin, Mark Diamond, Julia Durbin, Caroline Elliot, Graham Ellis, the late Chris Evans, Andrew Fullerton, Phil Hughes, Chris Kane, Margaret Mills, Peter Jefferson, Phil Hughes, Sir Nicholas Kenyon, Luke O'Shea, Bob Ogilvie, Robin Reynolds, Bill Rogers, Joanna Streeten, Joanne Sweeney and Geoff Walden. I should like to say a special thank you to Sir Terry Wogan for his wonderful foreword, and to three BBC staff members in particular, all of whom have devoted time and energy beyond the call of duty: Richard Jeffries, Guy Saich and the multi-talented Robert Seatter.

Also thanks to the Langham Hotel and the Yorkshire Grey Public House, the British Film Institute, the London Metropolitan Archive and the excellent Arthur Lloyd for photographs. I am indebted to Roger Beckwith, Robert Elwall, Bernie Evans, Julia Mackenzie, John Strubbe and Jenni Waugh.

I am particularly grateful to an immensely patient and talented publishing team at Merrell: Paul Arnot, Nicola Bailey, Kim Cope, Michelle Draycott, Rosanna Fairhead and Julian Honer. Thanks also to designers John Powner, Karishma Rafferty and Louisa Wood of Atelier Works; Alistair Layzell; Tim Crocker for his superb photographs; Alan Gardner for his conversation and progressive ukulele playing; and to my parents, Lyn and Robert.

Finally, and most importantly, thank you to Lucy Worsley for her encouragement and support. Above everyone, this book would simply not have happened without her.

Index

Page numbers in *italic* refer to the illustrations

Abramsky, Jenny 129, *142*
Acts of Inscribing (Furlong) 139, *141*
Adam, Robert 130
Adelaide House 81
air-conditioning 90–91, 98, 153
Air Ministry, Meteorological Department 12
air raids 102, 103, *103*, *104*, *108*
Alexandra Palace 86
All Souls Church 22, *119*
  and *Breathing* 139, *182*
  external lighting *138*
  MJP development plan *125*, *126*, 129, *129*, 130
  proposal to demolish 25–26
All Souls Primary School 139, *141*
Allen, Lady 48
Allies and Morrison 126
Alsop and Stormer *127*
announcers 15, *157*
Architectural Review 32, 33, 42, 48, 51, 53, 98, 119
Ariel, as metaphor for broadcasting 38
Ariel Hearing Celestial Music (Gill) *180*
Armonier, E. 38
Art Deco light fittings 44, *82–83*, *165*, *166*, *171*, *172*
artists' foyer 48–51, *81*
artists' lobby *168–69*
Asia House, Lime Street 22, *23*
Askey, Arthur 102
atrium 130
Audley Trust 29

Bagpuss *156*
Baird Television Company 92
Bakerloo line 98, 110, 131
Band Waggon 102
Bayes, Gilbert 82–84, *84*
BBC
  coat of arms 38, *160*
  digital services 124, 150
  early history 10–19
  Foster plans for new radio building *119*, *119*
  good causes 69
  light entertainment programmes 97
  listening numbers 15, 116
  motto 160–61
  Royal Charter 15, 142

  in Second World War 102–10
  SOS service 69
  souvenir guidebook 45, *46–47*
  staff numbers 17, 43–44, 97, 114
  Woodrooffe incident 101
BBC Audio and Music 9, *126*
BBC Dance Orchestra 34, 57
BBC Engineering Training Manual 102
'BBC Experience' 121
BBC Forces Programme 102
BBC Handbook 16–17, *16–17*, 33
BBC Listener Research Section 97–98
BBC Network Radio *171*
BBC News 9, 124, *126*
BBC Property 130
BBC Radio and Music 124
BBC Souvenir Book 54
BBC: The Voice of Britain 48, 52, 81
BBC World Service 9, 17, 124, *126*, 139
BBC Yearbook 16, 26, 34, 38–41, *38*, 42, 44, 50, 66, 97, 99, 118
BBC7 144
Beatl building board 34, *88*
Beecham, Sir Thomas 26
Belcher, John 22
Belfrage, Bruce 103, *103*
Bennett, Arnold 75
Berlin, Haus des Rundfunks 23
'Betterway' signage system *81*
Big Ben 15, *19*
birdsong recordings *19*
Birley, Oswald *160–61*
Birmingham 124
Birt, John 120, *121*
Blackburn, Tony 118, *118*
Blattnerphones 64, 65
Blitz (1940–41) 103–109, *103–108*
Blount, Edward 29
Blue Peter 139, *141*
boiler room 91
Bovis Lend Lease 131, 142
Bowie, David 121
Breathing (Plensa and MacCormac) 139, *182*
Brettenham House, London 41, *41*
Briggs, Asa 54
British Museum 130
British Thomson-Houston 12
Broadcasting House
  air-conditioning 90–91, 98, 153
  BBC moves into 34
  cabling 121, *153*, *162–63*

clocks 45
completion of first phase of redevelopment 142, *143*
confusing layout 44, 56
constraints of site 22, 24–25, 26, 42
construction 20–34, *30–31*
costs 24, 41
curved elevation 26–27, *27–29*
decoration 38, *180*
electricity consumption 91
energy efficiency 142
entrance *167*
entrance hall 48, 80, *166–67*
extensions
  BHX 116–18, *116*, 121
  BHXX 120
  east wing *182*, *186–87*
flag 38, *38*, 48
flowers 41, 48, *48*
Gill's sculptures 2, 29, *32*, 34, 38, *39*, 96, 97, *134*, 139, *180–81*
glazed façade *184–85*
Grade II listing 119, 124, 131
'heritage areas' 131
inscriptions *80*
lifts 51, *164–65*
lighting 44, 45, *82–83*, *165*, *166*, 171, *172*
materials 33–34, *34*
medical services 77
meeting-rooms 120–21
MJP development plan 124–30, *124–31*
nautical elements 41
in the 1930s 36–93
open-plan production floors *131*, *136–37*, 142, *150–51*
outside cleaned 116, *118*, 139
Phase Two 130, *186–87*
plant room *90–91*
preliminary designs 23–29, *24–25*
proposed extension 98–99, *99*, 103, 110
public art programme 139, *139–41*
public tours 44, 121
radio masts 38, *43*, *182*
reactions to 38–42
'Regent Street disease' 139
remodelling 131–39, *132–33*
restaurants 87, 116–18
royal opening 43
in Second World War 103–10, *103–108*, *110–11*
shop 121

signage 45, 81
space problems 98–99
staff 42, 43–44, 43, 48, 49, 77
staff complaints about building
    98–99, 114–16, 120–21
staircases 154–55
'street' 129
'stronghold' (air-raid shelter)
    110, 110
telephone exchange 63
time capsule 29
'Top Hat' design 22, 23, 26
war damage repaired 114, 114, 116
water consumption 91
windows 29, 41, 150, 180
see also concert hall, control
    rooms, libraries, studios and
    other individual rooms
Broadway House 41
Brookmans Park Transmitting
    Station 54
The Builder 42
Building the BBC: A Return to Form 126
Bush House 17, 81, 114, 124
Byron, Robert 42

Cain, John 98
Carr, Michael 8
Carrier Engineering Company 91
Carse, Duncan 109
Caterall Quartet 82
Catling, Brian 139
Central Council for Schools
    Broadcasting 98
Channel 4 headquarters 120
Chermayeff, Serge 32, 52, 57, 58,
    73, 147
Children's Hour 72, 89, 98
Chipperfield (David) Architects 126
Churchill, Winston 15
Civil Aviation Authority 139
Clarke, Tom 54
clocks 45, 85
Close Up 116
Cloth of Gold 141
Coates, Wells 32–33, 52, 54–55, 59,
    65, 68, 102, 148
colours
    green room 85
    remodelling of Broadcasting House
        135, 165
    rugs 34
    staircases 154–55
    studios 52, 57, 75, 88
    waiting-room 72
Commission for Architecture and
    the Built Environment 126
concert hall 44, 82–83
    bas-reliefs 82, 84
    green room 85
    organ 84, 99, 102, 102
    preliminary designs 24, 25
    refurbishment 116, 121, 135
    in Second World War 106–107,
        109
    soundproofing 99
    staff photographed in 43
    see also radio theatre
control rooms
    continuity suites 101, 102, 157
    dramatic control rooms 59–61,
        101

London control room 102, 116,
    162–63
    main control room 54–55
    music control room 62
Cooper, Tony 139
council chamber 78–79, 135, 160
Cox & Cardale 23–24
cue lights 59
Curie, Eve 103

Daily Express 29, 34
Daily Herald 97
Daily Mail 26, 54
daily service 75
dance (jazz) band studio 52, 89,
    92–93
Danziger, Nick 139
Daventry 15, 15
de Gaulle, Charles 102
Death at Broadcasting House 44, 56, 60
debates studio 58
Dell, Mark Oliver 9, 48, 49, 50
Denham, Maurice 165
Desert Island Discs 150, 156
Design Steering Group 129–30
digital services 124, 150
Director-General's office 70–72
Director of Programmes' office 69
Donnacona building board 34, 57, 72
Dorchester House, Park Lane 17, 19
Dorn, Marion 72
drama productions
    acoustic effects 148
    control rooms 59–61, 101
    drama studio 102, 115, 116
    dramatic control panels (DCPs)
        60–61
    dramatic effects studio 64, 65
    sound effects 60, 64–66, 86, 139
dressing-rooms 89, 176–77
Dutch Labour Party Broadcasting
    Station, Hilversum 23
Dyke, Greg 124, 129

echo rooms 86
Eckersley, Roger 16, 69
Edward VIII, King 15
eel grass, sound insulation 34
Egton House 114, 135
electricity consumption 91
Elizabeth, Queen Mother 100
Elizabeth II, Queen 100
    Christmas broadcasts 141
    coronation 116, 116–17
    opens first phase of
        redevelopment 142, 142, 166
Elmes, Simon 120
Eluard, Paul 169
Empire Service 53, 64, 87, 98
The End of Savoy Hill 44
engineers 15–16, 42, 43, 43
English Heritage 119, 130
Enter Shikari 171
entrance hall 48, 80, 166–67
Evening News 97
Evening Standard 34
Everett, Kenny 118, 118
Excess Baggage 150

FA Cup Final (1938) 101
fabrics
    dance (jazz) band studio 89

green room 85
rugs 34
vaudeville studio 88
Fair, J.W. 22
Farey, George 26–27
Fenton, James, Memorial 139
fireplaces 71, 79
Fletcher Priest 127
Foley, Lord 22
Foley House 70
The Food Programme 150
Foort, Reginald 84
Forces programme 102
Fortey, Eastland 86
Foster, Norman 119–20, 119, 124
Foster Father (Gill) 180–81
France, gift to BBC 169
French, Leslie 180
Fry, Stephen 171
Furlong, William, Acts of Inscribing
    139, 141
furniture 45, 68, 88, 135

General Electric 12
general office 77
General Strike (1926) 14, 15,
    110
George V, King 15, 15, 43, 44, 53,
    101, 166
George VI, King 100
Geraldo and His Orchestra 8
Gidley, Tom 139
Gielgud, Val 60–61, 148
Gill, Eric 9, 29, 32, 34, 139
    Ariel Hearing Celestial Music 180
    Foster Father 180–81
    Prospero and Ariel 2, 38, 39, 96, 97,
        134, 180–81, 181
    The Sower 80, 166–67
Glasgow 124
Gloag, John 73
Goatman, Wilfrid 48
Goldsmith, V.H. 32, 34, 53, 75
gramophone players 86
Gray, George Kruger 160
green room 85
Greenwich Time Signal 15, 54
Grisewood, Freddie 92, 98, 109, 114

Hall, Henry 34, 52, 57, 89, 101
Handley, Tommy 102, 102
Hardy, Oliver 58
Harley Street Conservation Area
    129
Haselden, Ron 139
Hastings, Hubert de Cronin 32
Haus des Rundfunks, Berlin 23
Hawkins, Jane Ellen 116
Hendy, David 118
Hill, Vernon 75, 104
Hilversum, Dutch Labour Party
    Broadcasting Station 23
Holden, Charles 41, 53
Home Service 102
    see also World Service
Hopton-Wood stone 80, 164–65
Houses of Parliament 16, 110
Howard de Walden estate 29
Hubble, Margaret 109
Humphrys, John 120, 142
Hunt, W. & E. 41
Huntingdon, John 18

In Our Time 150
In Tune 142, 147
The Independent 121
Independent Television News 119
Information & Archives department
    142, 178–79
Institute of Electrical Engineers 13
Internet 124
It's That Man Again (ITMA) (radio
    programme) 102
ITV 116

Jefferson, Peter 157
Johnston, Brian 114–16
Joseph, Ernest 41

Keats, John 82–84
Kerfuffle (Rideal) 139, 140

Land Securities 142
Langham, Sir James 22
Langham Hotel 22, 42, 114, 119
Langham Street pedestrian space
    139, 139, 186
Laurel, Stan 58
Lawson Dick, Clare 103–109, 104
Lewis, C. J. 77
libraries 76
    Information & Archives
        department 142, 178–79
    music library 67, 103, 144, 178–79
    seventh-floor library 147
Library 'talks' studio 73, 75
lifts 51, 164–65
lighting 45
    Art Deco fittings 44, 82–83, 165,
        166, 171, 172
    concert hall 82–83
    external 138, 139
    radio theatre 172
    remodelling of Broadcasting
        House 135
Lincrusta wallpaper 34, 89
Lipton, Stuart 126
The Listener 41, 103, 180
listening-rooms 86, 101, 102
London City Airport 139
London control room 102, 116,
    162–63
London County Council 25–26, 29
London Metropolitan Archives 131
London Underground 53, 110, 120,
    131, 135
Long Acre studio 92
Lucas, Matt 171
Lurçat, Jean, The Poet 169
Lynn, Vera 102

MacCarthy, Fiona 180
MacCormac, Sir Richard 126–29,
    126, 139, 142, 182
MacCormac Jamieson Prichard
    124–31, 126–30, 139, 142
McCormick, Reverend Pat 38
McGrath, Raymond 32, 44, 102
    council chamber 78–79
    dance band studio 52
    importance of Broadcasting House
        to industrial design 52
    listening-rooms 86
    office of the Director of
        Programmes 69

restaurant 87
studio walls 34
vaudeville studio 33, 51, 88
Macgregor, L.D. 109
MacPherson, Sandy 102, 102
Magnet House, Kingsway 12, 43, 67
Maida Vale studios 97, 99, 101, 114
Malinowski, Antoni 135
Manchester 124
Marconi 12
Marconi Stille system 64
Marshall & Tweedy 114
Mary, Queen 44, 166
Marylebone Borough Council 25
Maschwitz, Eric 60, 97
Maufe, Edward 33, 74–75, 104
Melba, Dame Nellie 12, 12
Memorial (Fenton) 139
Meteorological Department,
    Air Ministry 12
Metropolitan-Vickers 12
Metropolitan Water Board 30
microphones 68
Midweek 150
military band studio 57
Milne, Alistair 120
Mitcheson, George Gibson 97
Modus Operandi 139
Mollison, Jim 92
Montagu's 23–24
Montgomery, Field Marshal 110, 111
Moreland Hayne and Company 30
Munroe, Mr (Studio Executive) 81
Murdoch, Richard 102
Murray, Jenni 151
music
    listening-rooms 86
    music control room 62
    music library 67, 103, 144, 178–79
    see also concert hall
Music While You Work 102

Nash, John 22, 26, 130
Nelson, HMS 101
New Statesman 98
New York, Radio City 23
news studios 68
newsroom 129

Ogilvie, Frederick 109
Old Glamis Fabrics 78–79
Olympic Games (1948) 116
On Air (public art) 139, 141
organ, concert hall 84, 99, 102, 102
Orwell, George 110, 139
outside broadcasts 15, 98, 162

Paramount Astoria Girls 92
Parry (Eric) Architects 127
Patts, Joe 73
Payne, Jack 57, 99
Peel, John 178
Perry, Fred 92
Pevsner, Nikolaus 41
Pimlott, Mark, World 139, 139
Piranesi, Giovanni Battista 82
plant room 90–91
Plensa, Jaume, Breathing 139, 182
The Poet (Lurçat) 169
Portland, Duke of 22
Portland Place
    acquisition of site 22, 23

BBC acquires more buildings in 97, 98
constraints of site 22, 24–25, 26
Foster design for new radio building 119, 119
history of 22
landmine explodes in 109
proposed extension to Broadcasting House 98–99, 99
Portland stone 29, 30
Portsoken House, Minories 22, 23
Posford, George 48
Post Office 12, 44, 48, 81
Presence (video) 139
production offices 101, 131, 136–37, 150–51
Proms 80
Prospero and Ariel (Gill) 2, 38, 39, 96, 97, 134, 180–81, 181
Prudential Assurance Co. 116
Public Art Group 135, 139
public art programme 139, 139–41, 182
Punch 54

Queen's Hall 23, 26, 38, 80

radio
    digital services 124, 150
    expansion of services 118
    numbers of listeners 15, 116
    radio circles 16, 18, 69
Radio 1 118, 118, 178
Radio 3 142, 144, 147, 156, 162
Radio 4 142, 144, 147, 157
Radio City, New York 23
Radio Communication Company 12
Radio Luxembourg 97
Radio News 121
Radio Normandie 97
radio theatre 82–83, 121, 130, 135, 144, 170–77
    see also concert hall
Radio Times 8, 98, 99, 101, 116
Rae, Fiona, Signal 139, 141
Rasmussen, Steen Eiler 22
Read, Herbert 29
reception area 48, 80, 166–67
recording equipment 64, 64, 65
Regent Street 22, 25, 184
'Regent Street disease' 139
Reid, Colin 48, 98–99, 109, 120
Reilly, Charles 41, 42, 70, 77, 82
Reith, Sir John (Lord Reith) 12, 43, 48, 54, 97, 153
    on BBC as a living organism 43, 126
    and design of Broadcasting House 26, 29
    dislikes Broadcasting House 98
    entrance hall dedication 80
    and independence of BBC 15
    influence lingers in Broadcasting House 118
    leaves Savoy Hill 34, 35, 43
    office 70–71
    portrait of 160–61
    relationship with his staff 43, 98
    at Savoy Hill 13, 17
religious studio 33, 74–75, 104
REM 121
Rendall, Dr Montague 32, 80
Renishaw family 53

restaurants 87, 116–18
Reynolds News 97
Richards, J.M. 41, 53
Richman, Martin 139
Riddy, John 139
Rideal, Liz, Kerfuffle 139, 140
Robertson, Sir Howard 116
Robinson, H. Fitzroy 116
Rogers, Richard 120
Room 101 (Whiteread) 139, 139
Royal Academy 9, 120
Royal Fine Art Commission 99
Royal Institute of British Architects (RIBA) 22, 29
Royal Navy 101
Royal Opera House 130

St George's Hall 97, 103
Salter, Lionel 98–99
Savoy Hill 13, 14, 19, 43, 98
    BBC moves out of 34, 35, 44
    expansion of 17
    studios 13, 17, 18, 32, 33, 52
Second World War 101, 102–10, 102–108, 139, 166, 169
Selfridges 13
Senate House 41, 41
Shakespeare, William 38, 84, 180–81
Shell-Mex House 41, 41
Sheppard Robson 142
signage 45, 81
Signal (Rae) 139, 141
Simpson, John 118
Skelly, Ian 156
Smith, John 126
solar shield 183
Solomon, Robert 22, 26
SOS service 69
sound effects 60, 64–66, 86, 139
The Sower (Gill) 80, 166–67
Spithead Review (1937), Woodrooffe incident 101
staircases 154–55
Stanton Williams 127
The Star 99
Start the Week 150
stone
    Hopton-Wood stone 80, 164–65
    Portland stone 29, 30
    'Regent Street disease' 139
'stronghold' (air-raid shelter) 110, 110
Studio Decoration Committee 53, 75
studios
    acoustics 33–34, 34, 116, 132
    announcing-rooms 72
    continuity studios 101, 102, 157
    control desks 158–59
    design of Broadcasting House 29–34, 31
    dramatic control panels (DCPs) 60–61
    duty announcers 101
    furniture 68
    listening-rooms 101, 102
    Long Acre studio 92
    Maida Vale studios 97, 99, 101, 114
    Marconi House 12–13, 18
    microphones 68
    new methods of controlling programmes 101–102

news-agency tape machines 68
    production rooms 101
    proposed extension to Broadcasting House 99
    redevelopment plan 126, 131, 132, 146–49, 156–57
    religious studios 33, 74–75, 102, 104
    at Savoy Hill 13, 17, 18, 32, 33, 52
    'self-operation studios' 157
    soundproofing 24, 25, 34, 98, 132
    staff complaints about 98–99
    Studio 3A (Children's Hour) 72, 89, 102
    Studio 3B ('Talks') 73
    Studio 3C ('Talks') 73
    Studio 3D (Library 'talks' studio) 73, 75
    Studio 3E (religious studio) 74–75, 102, 104
    Studio 4A (news studio) 68, 121
    Studio 4B (news studio) 68, 157
    Studio 6A (drama studio) 102, 115, 116
    Studio 6D (dramatic effects studio) 64, 65
    Studio 8A (military band studio) 57, 102, 116, 120
    Studio 8B (debates studio) 58
    Studio 40B (continuity studio) 157
    Studio 60A (drama studio) 148–49
    Studio 80A 146–47
    Studio BA (vaudeville studio) 33, 51, 88, 99, 102
    Studio BB (dance [jazz] band) studio 52, 89, 92–93, 102
    studio control cubicles 101
    Studio Decoration Committee 32
    'talks' studios 33, 73, 75, 102
    ventilation 90–91, 98
    war damage 103, 109
    woffices 153
    Woman's Hour 156, 158–59
    see also concert hall; control rooms
Sturgess, Olive 18

'talks' studios 33, 73, 75, 102
tape recorders 64, 65
telephone exchange 63
television
    first broadcasts 92–93, 116
    licences 44, 116
Television Centre, White City 116, 121, 124
Thames, River 15, 15
Thinking Allowed 150
Thomson, Leo 141
'Three Musketeers' 32–33
The Times 12
Today 120, 121
transmitters, early history 12, 15, 15
Tudsbery, Marmaduke 8, 17, 80
    preliminary designs 22–25, 29
    proposed extension 99
    studio design 32
    ventilation system 91
    and war damage 103, 114

Ukelele Orchestra of Great Britain 147
Unilever House 81

Val Myer, George 8, 22, 120
    background 22
    and Broadcasting House windows 29, 41
    concert hall 82–83
    and criticism of Broadcasting House 42
    decorations 180
    designs BBC coat of arms 38
    designs extension 99
    entrance hall 48, 80
    MJP development plan and 126, 129, 130, 131
    preliminary designs 23–29, 24–25
    'Top Hat' design 22, 23
    use of Hopton-Wood stone 164–65
vaudeville studio 33, 51, 88, 99, 102
Vaughan, PC John Charles 109
ventilation 90–91, 98, 153
Victoria and Albert Museum 139
Victoria line 135

Wainwright, H.L. 9, 48, 49, 50
waiting-room 72, 147
Walker, Allen 16
Warren Trotter, Dorothy 33, 75
Washington, George 75
water
    'Regent Street disease' 139
    water consumption 91
Watson-Hart, Francis James 22
Waygood-Otis 165
weather forecasts 12, 15
Welch, Elizabeth 103
Wellesley, Lord Gerald 48, 52, 73, 75
Wembley Stadium 116
Western Electric 12
Westminster City Council 130, 139
White City 116, 119, 121, 124
Whiteread, Rachel, Room 101 139, 139
Wilder, Ian 130
Wimperis, Simpson & Guthrie 99
Winchester, Marchioness of 29
wireless clubs 16, 18, 69
Wireless Magazine 26
woffices 153
Wogan, Sir Terry 6, 7, 120, 142
Woman's Hour 150–51, 156, 158–59
women's dressing-room 89
Wood, Robert 16
Woodrooffe, Lieutenant-Commander Thomas 100, 101
World (Pimlott) 139, 139
World Service 9, 17, 124, 126, 139
    see also Home Service
Wyatt, James 22, 29, 70

Yass, Catherine 139
Yentob, Alan 129
You and Yours 150
Young, Kirsty 156

First published 2008 by Merrell
Publishers Limited

81 Southwark Street
London SE1 0HX

merrellpublishers.com

in association with

BBC
Broadcasting House
London W1A 1AA

bbc.co.uk

British Library Cataloguing-in-
Publication Data
Hines, Mark
The story of Broadcasting House:
Home of the BBC
1. Broadcasting House – History
2. British Broadcasting Corporation –
History
I. Title II. Crocker, Tim
725.2'3

ISBN-13: 978-1-8589-4421-0
ISBN-10: 1-8589-4421-X

Produced by
Merrell Publishers Limited
Designed by
Atelier Works
Copy-edited by
Elizabeth Tatham
Proof-read by
Sarah Yates
Indexed by
Hilary Bird

Printed and bound in China

Jacket, front Broadcasting House
photographed at twilight on
31 October 2007 by Tim Crocker.
Jacket, back Broadcasting House then
and now *(top to bottom, left to right)*:
the building from the south; Eric Gill's
statue *Prospero and Ariel* over the
entrance; the radio theatre (originally
the concert hall); the builders at
work; the old sound-effects room
and the modern *Woman's Hour*
studio; variety programming; the
entrance hall; Broadcasting House,
All Souls Church and Portland Place.
Frontispiece Prospero and Ariel,
Eric Gill's iconic sculpture over the
entrance to Broadcasting House.

Picture Credits
*l = left; r = right; t = top; b = bottom;
c = centre*
Will Alsop: 127*br*
British Broadcasting Corporation/
Anna Gordon: back cover *l (all), cl (top),
cr (all), r (except top and bottom)*, 7, 8,
12–17, 18*t*, 18*br*, 19*tl, tcl, tcr, tr*, 22,
23*l*, 24*r*, 25–32, 33*t, bl*, 34–35, 38–40,
41*l*, 42–50, 53–89, 91–93, 96–97, 98*r*,
99*r*, 100–108, 110–11, 114–18, 120,
124–25, 132–35, 142, 156*br*, 171
© Tony Cooper and Martin
Richman: 38
Tim Crocker: jacket front, jacket back
cl (except top), r (top and bottom),
2, 4, 136–37, 143, 145–155, 156*l, tr*,
157–72, 174–87
© Rod Dorling: 141*l, cl*
English Heritage: 19*b*
Fletcher Priest: 127*tl*
Foster and Partners: 119
gmj: 139*b*
Mark Hines: 23, 24*c*, 41*tr, cr*
London Metropolitan Archive: 24*l*,
98*l*, 99*l*
MacCormac Jamieson Prichard
Architects: 121, 126, 128–31
Eric Parry Architects: 127*bl*
Andrew Putler: 127*tr*
RIBA: 33*br*, 51, 52
© Liz Rideal: 140
Courtesy of the Timothy Taylor
Gallery, London: 141*l*
Courtesy of the V&A Museum and
Gagosian Gallery, London: 139*t*
Lucy Worsley: 41*br*

The author and publisher have
made every effort to trace copyright
holders of the illustrations reproduced
in this book; they will be happy to
correct in subsequent editions any
errors or omissions that are brought
to their attention.

This publication was made possible
by generous support from:

Bickerdike Allen Partners

FABER MAUNSELL | AECOM

The guiding principle was to exploit to the utmost the peculiar advantages in
I tried to make full use of the gracious horizontal lines which this cu
of harmony with anything in the neighbourhood that I am not able to gi
of hard labour since the joint report plans were prepared have obviousl
plain front? The BBC now had to contemplate a building into which they c
are deprived of sleep all night because of the unceasing and excruciating noi
materials and their application must be explored Brain centre of modern
factor since Caxton first introduced his printing press into England? A worth
in here We called it the Big House My lasting impression was that it w
of the larger world outside with vibrations reaching out to the farthest island
of the building, isolated from all the rest, where the makers of the noises p
has been washed away … Such a phenomenon has never occurred before in
appreciate. The microphone has provided a new means for distributing opini
sightless, cheering the bedridden. The lighthouse watchers, men who brav
the strain of those who live in loneliness or pain. There is no doubt tha
no means reached its limits Visualize a few of the people whom you know
with them … Let your voice play about as it normally would, and make
broadcasting was invented nobody had ever had such opportunities for bo
a little space and without faithless gloom with joy upon thy face pray for
not sure if the BBC could live up to it I'm so dazzled I can't even thin
accompanied by a veritable tornado of air blast To someone like myself,
importance, the general trend of the moment is a little disheartening Endle
holes in the carpet covered with gaffer tape, air conditioning, cold in win
broadcasting to a brick wall without ever seeing daylight. Happy days! It
hold on – there's a Tube going past!' and wait till the rumble stopped! Br
swing to her petticoats than before Love the new spaces at the top A really
space to work Utterly inspiring Great colour An amazing building Fant